BREADCRAFT

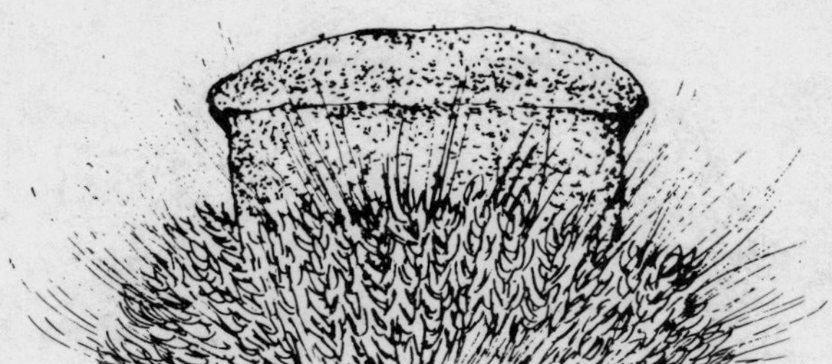

BY CHARLES & VIOLET SCHAFER

ILLUSTRATED BY BARNEY WAN

YERBA BUENA PRESS

SAN FRANCISCO

1974

ISBN 0-912738-04-9

Library of Congress Card #73-20569
Printed in The United States Of America

666 & 651 Howard St.
San Francisco, California 94105

First Edition

Distributed By Random House, Inc.
and in Canada By Random House of Canada, Ltd.
ISBN 0-394-70635-8

About the authors

Coauthors Charles and Violet Schafer worked as a team before their marriage 25 years ago. Asked how he would describe his wife for a stranger, Mr. Schafer said, "She's a poet." The term, he said, explained her consuming interest in language more directly than did professional titles of positions she has held in the West and Midwest. Titles embrace art columnist, radio script writer, director of public relations for public and private schools, teacher, airline publications editor and author of *Herbcraft* and *Eggcraft.*

Mr. Schafer himself is a conference consultant who has devoted the last 15 years exclusively to contributing to the literature and practice of conference methods and techniques. He just happens to have a connoisseur's interest in cooking and baking. In the 20 years immediately following his graduation from Stanford, he was associated with two international companies at the management level in New York, San Francisco and the Orient. His culinary experiences in the Orient were reflected in *Wokcraft* which he coauthored with his wife. He enthusiastically tested the breads in *Breadcraft* and contributed the spirit of play evident in its pages.

About the illustrator

Illustrator Barney Wan brings a cosmopolitan background to his drawings for *Breadcraft.* Born in Hong Kong, he received his early education there and in Canton. He continued his studies at City College of San Francisco, earning a degree in commercial and fine arts and winning scholarships to Stephens Art Institute and California School of Fine Arts. He became known for his exciting fashion illustrations for leading San Francisco stores and showed water colors and paintings in San Francisco exhibitions.

During the last 14 years he has worked abroad in France and England. In Paris he did illustrations for *Elle,* French *Vogue,* and *Marie-Claire* and worked with a number of advertising agencies.

From 1968 to 1973, he was art director for British *Vogue.* Currently free lancing, he is experimenting and also "searching for the essence of life."

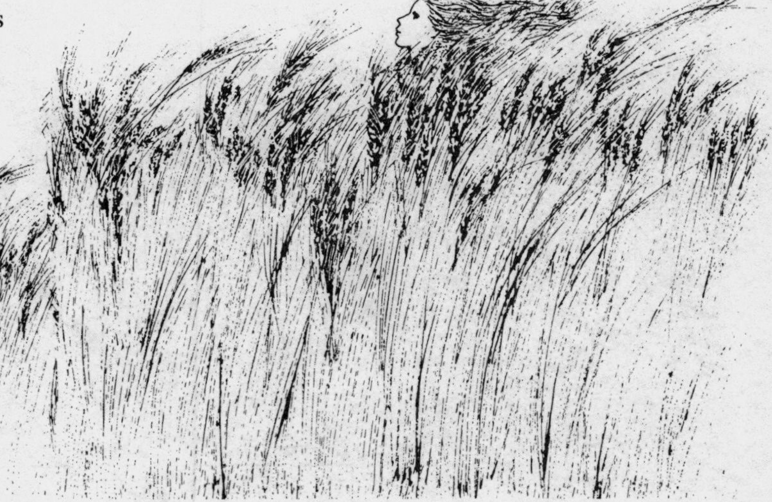

CONTENTS

FOREWORD

A REWARDING STUDY

This has been a happy occupation looking through one hundred year old cook books and learning how grandmother and great grandmother baked bread; seeking out breads wherever we traveled and returning home to try our hand at re-creating the best tasting, the most imaginative; exchanging bread recipes with new friends and old; crossing cultures and sharing bread traditions with people from backgrounds different from our own; and experimenting with many kinds of bread stuffs and devising new recipes.

WHAT IF . . .?

Bread as culture and bread as food have posed engrossing questions. What if, we asked ourselves, what if we added a handful of fresh pineapple mint or a teaspoon of powdered rosemary to a cake bread? What kind of bread recipes make good hamburger buns? Does the recipe really mean we should bake this bread in a coffee can? Can we make a bread in a hurry, or if we can't do that, is there a way to mix now and bake later? If we make a lot, can we freeze it and keep it if we don't want to show off and give it away? How far can we go in experimenting with ingredients? And on and on!

SYMPATHY'S SUSTAINING BREAD

Any preoccupation with bread is bound to disclose its awesome character.

Our Puritan fathers judged brown bread and the Gospel to be good fare. This pairing is common. Reverence for bread has been especially strong in rural societies and Catholic countries. One did not commit the sacrilege of wasting bread.

An Irishman who throws a crust into the ashes risks, before he dies, having to follow a crow seven miles in the hope the bird will drop such a crust to him.

If bread drops on the floor in Spain or Belgium, householders pick it up, kiss it and return it to table to help a soul escape purgatory, they say.

In old Ukraine, bread was one of the holiest of foods. Among the older people, even leftovers are still handled carefully. If it is dropped to the floor, it is picked up reverently, kissed in apology before being returned to table or placed where birds can make a meal of it.

Bread is always placed on a covered table. One never eats it with his hat on. And there was a time when the baking of bread began with the sign of the cross to venerate the labor that produced the loaves.

So the bread we bring you now is more than bread.

Violet and Charles Schafer

DEMETER

SYMPATHY'S SUSTAINING BREAD

Any preoccupation with bread is bound to disclose its awesome character.

Our Puritan fathers judged brown bread and the Gospel to be good fare. This pairing is common. Reverence for bread has been especially strong in rural societies and Catholic countries. One did not commit the sacrilege of wasting bread.

An Irishman who throws a crust into the ashes risks, before he dies, having to follow a crow seven miles in the hope the bird will drop such a crust to him.

If bread drops on the floor in Spain or Belgium, householders pick it up, kiss it and return it to table to help a soul escape purgatory, they say.

In old Ukraine, bread was one of the holiest of foods. Among the older people, even leftovers are still handled carefully. If it is dropped to the floor, it is picked up reverently, kissed in apology before being returned to table or placed where birds can make a meal of it.

Bread is always placed on a covered table. One never eats it with his hat on. And there was a time when the baking of bread began with the sign of the cross to venerate the labor that produced the loaves.

So the bread we bring you now is more than bread.

Violet and Charles Schafer

DEMETER

THE RARE & CURIOUS STORY OF A COMMON FOOD

IN THE BEGINNING

Anyone who has ever stood up to his shoulders in a field of ripened wheat as I have and watched a warm summer wind play over a great stand of the grain must admit to a sense of awe.

This is the golden hoard that is the beginning of man's most important food – bread – even as it was thousands of years ago.

The first man to eat wheat stripped the kernels from the grasses in the field just as farm children do today and chewed "wheat gum." Centuries passed before he freed the grain from its outer covering to grind flour for bread. For centuries more, porridge and flat bread were the products of his labor.

It was 75,000 years ago, they say, that man first ground seeds to make a rough meal. Only 12,000 years ago man made rubbing stones and crude mortars to grind the seeds. Ten thousand years ago, the Oak Grove Indians of California were making paste and meal from a mixture of acorns, beechnuts and lily seeds.

In the same age, as remains of primitive barley and one-grained wheat cakes show, Swiss Lake Dwellers began to develop the art of baking. To prepare their cakes, they crushed grain and nuts upon a stone with a second, fist-size round stone. After soaking, the crushed cereal was flattened into cakes and left to dry in the sun or bake on hot stones or in hot ashes.

This was the primitive way man prepared his cereal foods for a long, long time.

BETTER BREAD THROUGH CHEMISTRY

It is a moot point who first made bread – the Chinese or the Egyptians. Very early the Chinese knew the secret of fermenting doughs and producing something entirely new by applying heat. Their style was to steam the bread as they do to this very day.

For whatever reason, we have more information about Egyptian bread makers. While the rest of the world was making do with flat bread and porridge, they were fermenting dough 5,000 years ago. Bread was their principal food and they made it much as we do today. Well preserved loaves discovered in the pyramids testify to this.

According to their legends, Isis, Lady of Bread and Goddess of Fertility, found wheat and barley in the wild. Her husband, Osiris, took the wild grains a step farther and fostered their cultivation by his peoples. Sprouting grain signified immortality. Grain stuffed effigies of Osiris were emblematic of resurrection in Egyptian tombs.

OBSERVED BUT NOT UNDERSTOOD

The Egyptians carried bread making to perfection. Their bakers used the yeast produced in brewing beer to ferment and leaven bread doughs. It was a mystery to them how it worked. They simply observed that when they baked their sour dough, something wonderful, something entirely new resulted. They observed, too, that they could not achieve this new thing in the old ways. So these people whose priests were chemists and spent their days mixing and brewing invented the first oven.

The cylindrical affairs made from bricks of Nile clay looked like beehives. They made it possible to bake bread evenly, thoroughly, and in quantity.

AN OLD EGYPTIAN SECRET

Before baking the dough, they salted it and kneaded it thoroughly, sometimes with their feet – a practice, incidentally, that persisted into modern times in Scotland.

In time, they discovered they could reserve a bit of dough from one batch to start the next dough on its way to bubbling and rising. This was the first "starter" which you can now purchase in dry form for a nominal sum. For a few coins, as it were, you can buy an old Egyptian secret!

Besides their discovery of fermentation processes and the usefulness of "starters"; besides their invention of the oven, these sophisticated bakers were the first to devise papyrus sieves for milling. This permitted separating finer flour from course, dark meals.

BREAD STUFFS IN ANCIENT EGYPT

For their bread, the Egyptians used wheat; spelt, a cereal closely allied to both wheat and barley and at one time the chief cereal of ancient Egypt; barley; and durra, a variety of millet. Barley is thought to be the earliest.

With these bread stuffs, ingenious bakers provided their countrymen with great variety. The rich had white bread made from wheat flour. Those below them ate barley bread. Those on the bottom rung of the ladder lived almost exclusively on coarse durra bread.

ARTISTIC VARIATIONS ON THE THEME

Bakers also exercised considerable artistry. Basic breads were baked in jars and molds which were heated beforehand, but breads also came in cubes with domes, high cones and braids. They came in the shapes of pyramids, fish and birds. Among their bread molds was one of Hathor, the divine cow. Breads were small and round like muffins or

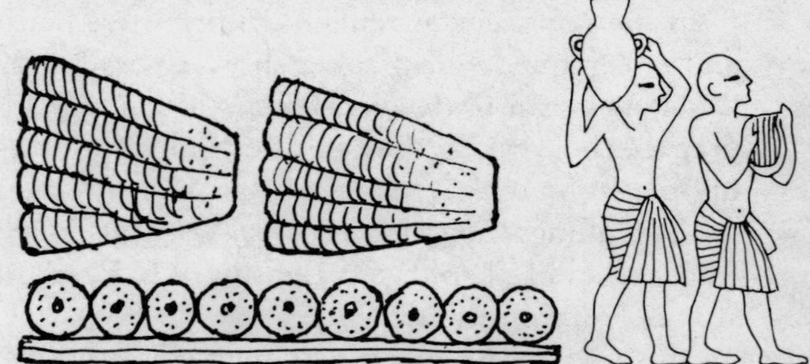

hard rolls. They came in long loaves, too, sprinkled with seeds like today's Vienna bread.

As many as 50 varieties of bread came to table in early Egypt. A single feast would tantalize banqueters with 20 kinds at a sitting.

BREAD IN THE HEREAFTER

Murals in Egyptian tombs carried many symbols. One, describing a king's assets, is a graphic picture of the royal bakery. We see men treading dough in a large trough; bearing water in large jars; kneading bread at a table; setting molded dough in heated dishes; filling an oven first with fuel, then with small, uniform loaves.

Besides murals, there were funerary furnishings in the tombs. They included statuettes of bakers to serve the king after death. There was in the grave the *Book of the Dead* to guide the departed, to help help him get along in his new situation and counteract hostile influences.

Bread offerings were common. To protect them, the *Book of the Dead* recommended a magic spell.

I am a man who has bread in Heliopolis,
My bread is in Heaven with the Sun God,
My bread is on earth with Keb.
The boat of evening and of morning
Brings me the bread that is my meat
From the House of the Sun God.

BREAD ECONOMY

Egyptians based their administrative system on bread. They paid bills and wages with bread. A temple official could expect, in a year, 360 jugs of beer, 900 fine wheat breads and 36,000 flat breads.

Laborers received two jugs of beer and four loaves of durra for a day's work.

More than 3,000 years ago, bread as pay inspired what sounds like a curiously contemporary incident. In the reign of Ramses IX, workmen, denied their bread by their employer, engaged in a strike until their demands met favorable action from the Governor of Thebes. The price — or bribe — for a helpful official was also bread. He was paid two chests of bread for his assistance.

BREAD HAS BEEN MANY THINGS

In Egypt, the bread that kept man alive was intimately associated with his religious beliefs, his superstitions, folklore and his history and economy. These associations have been a continuing thread in many cultures.

In Biblical times, bread was a staple article of diet for the Hebrews. Every home in Chaldaea had an oven and grinding stones in its courtyard. Housewives made both leavened and unleavened bread.

Bread was the starting point of religious and social observances. There was a ritual exhibition of bread in the Jewish Tabernacle. Unleavened bread was eaten at Passover as it still is.

BREAD AS LUXURY

In ancient Greece and Rome, bread was both a staple and a luxury. Rich townsmen enjoyed a variety: poppyseed bread; hot rolls; breads both leavened and unleavened.

Bread stuffs included rice, barley, whole wheat and pulse. Breads were baked with suet, lard, cheese, honey, milk and oil.

Techniques varied. Breads were baked in ovens and fried on griddles. They were roasted on coals, in ashes and on spits. Some had the shapes of mushrooms or of flowers. They were sprinkled with aniseed and sesame. They were flavored with cumin and pepper. Some had almonds or hazelnuts. Some came in layers and probably looked like English cottage loaves still being made.

CELEBRATION OF BREAD

The Greeks celebrated bread in their observances for the Bread Church of Eleusis. Each September a nine-day celebration programmed processions, secret ceremonies, and rites in honor of the corn and bread goddess, Demeter.

Prominent in the processions was a chest bearer who carried cult objects — a baked plow of wheat and honey and other objects also made of bread dough.

Present, too, was a basket bearer who was to receive the first grains of the harvest.

Among the humblest were those who paraded bearing sheaves of grain, milling tools and big loaves of bread.

Greek bakers were important enough to stand for election as senators. As early as the 4th Century B.C., they made Athens famous for a banquet bread which was baked on a brazier and eaten folded and dipped in wine to restore flagging appetites. They catered to the Athenian taste for delicate white bread which remained a luxury item even into the 18th Century in Europe.

The Greeks not only brought bread to the Romans but were an early source of expert bakers when bread became important to them.

AND, LO! A GODDESS FOR THE OVEN!

Called "the Americans of their day," the Romans were the first measurably to advance the art of milling by applying rotary motion. Their clever milling machines ground grain between two circular stones, one turning and the other stationary. Large hour-glass mills, turned by animals or teams of slaves, and smaller portable querns spread throughout the Roman Empire.

They insulated hot air in their baking ovens and developed draft mechanisms and methods of holding ashes and introducing containers for water to encourage a fine crust on their loaves. They set up stone tables for preparing dough.

Even as they were bending their energies to such practical inventions, they were also acknowledging the mystery and the magic of the oven by holding festivals in honor of Fornax, Goddess of the Oven. To her, they dedicated the national observance, the Fornacalia. The annual festival took place June 9. On that day, bakers wreathed their ovens and baking utensils with flowers and they feasted.

ADVANCING THE ART

Roman inventions that made large scale milling practical as well as the official issue of doles of bread raised the status of the milling and baking industries. Bakers organized. They advanced their art enough to be able to assess the suitability of a grain for a particular kind of bread.

Romans altered milling processes in order to produce breads of different types and shapes to please consumers in all walks of life. Their expertise came at a time agriculture was improving and wheat was coming forward as the main crop in Southern Europe.

ROMAN BREAD STUFFS

Roman bakers imported honey from Greece and Asia Minor, oil from North Africa. They used rice, milk, cheese, sesame seeds, almonds, peppers, anise and laurel leaves.

The first Roman bread bakers had been housewives who made bread of siligo wheat. But as wives of the conquerors of the world, they retired from this low activity. Not until Rome was 600 years old, however, did public bakeries supply cities and raise baking to an art.

Bakery owners were chiefly freed slaves but highly respected. The first professionals were Greeks who taught the Romans what they knew. Syrians and Phoenicians were also avidly courted as apprentices because they had a sense of taste and had sensitive hands for the work.

BREAD AND HONORS

When bakers' guilds sprang up, the Roman state protected their rights. The baker who delivered good bread was deemed worthy of public offices. A member of the baker's guild was, in fact, the second mayor of Pompeii.

Another baker became a very wealthy man whose tomb memorialized the art of baking with bas reliefs. They depicted grain being brought and paid for; horses and mules working mills; men sifting bran from flour by hand; bakers forming loaves, loading dome-shaped ovens, weighing baskets of baked bread and carrying them off on their backs.

During the Republic, aediles supervised bakeries. Public granaries received grain and distributed it to bakers. Slaves ground the grain and when they won their freedom from Constantine, bakers recruited criminals for the task.

By 100 B.C., Rome had 258 bakeries. From Rome, the art spread throughout the Empire once Trajan had established his college of millers and bakers.

CONSPICUOUS CONSUMPTION

As with so many things, the Romans performed with conspicuous flare as bakers. There were bakers whose apprentices were said to wear gloves and gauze masks to prevent sweat or bad breath from affecting the dough. The dough itself yielded rare entertainment. Besides the ordinary bread, shaped like a bomb, they made bread on a spit and baked it in earthen vessels. Should a poet be guest of honor in a rich household, the bread would appear in the shape of a lyre. Wedding celebrations prompted bakers to make breads shaped like joined rings.

EARLY BREAD LINES

When Romans were bloated with power and the peoples in its capital city degenerated into wretchedness, rulers studied how to relieve poverty and

amuse the idle. So what had been monthly distributions of corn were converted into daily allowances of bread.

Authorities caused many ovens to be built and maintained at public expense. At an appointed hour, Roman citizens bearing tickets mounted a flight of steps set aside for citizens who enjoyed the same position and exchanged their tickets for a loaf of bread weighing three pounds.

BREAD INVASION

The Romans introduced bread to Europe where wheat culture had already begun. While Roman milling and baking operations had been unified, the practice in the North was to banish the mill to the outskirts of towns. This came about because milling had progressed to water and wind power. The separation was inimical to the millers. They fell into disfavor, not only with townsfolk but also with the bakers.

A LORDLY PREROGATIVE

In medieval England, baking was a home project. The lord of the manor whose prerogative it was to build the mills rented the mills to the millers who ground the flour to make the bread. And everyone who had grain to grind was forced to use the lord's mill. No one could grind his grain at home or harbor there a milling machine.

When the time came that bakers were established in the towns, they baked the flour householders brought to them. In time, they provided the flour and the bakery as we know it came into being.

OATS, PEASE, BEANS AND BARLEY GROW!

The predominant grain crop was rye. So the staple bread was rye for the laboring class. When rye was not in good supply, it was eked out with flour or meal made of oats, pease, beans and sometimes acorns. There was also wheaten bread or "maslin" – a mixture of wheat and rye. This the more prosperous enjoyed.

CLASS CONSCIOUS BREAD

In Elizabethan times, four loaves were commonly made – manchet, cheat, celsus and cibarus. Manchet, the best, was a white, 6-ounce loaf of well sifted flour. Cheat was a 1-pound wheaten loaf made of flour from which much of the bran was removed. Celsus was whole wheat bread. Cibarus, a very poor loaf, was "appointed in all times for servants, slaves, and the inferior type of people to feed upon."

Every rank had its appointed bread and an appointed amount of it. By the middle of the 18th Century, this class consciousness of bread had disappeared. White bread was ascendant as the diet of all. The cause lay in improvements in agriculture and in certain economic pressures on milling and marketing.

SETTING A FAIR PRICE

In 1155, bakers were forming guilds in Britain. In 1266, an act of Parliament regulated prices of English bread. Officials determined price by adding a sum to the price of flour to cover a baker's expenses and profit. An earlier edict of King John tied bread prices to grain prices. This was the oldest English price law. It allowed a baker to net a profit of 13 per cent.

IT IS THE LAW!

Bakers sold bread only by weight, except for fancy breads and rolls which were not clearly defined.

The law required bakers and sellers of bread to use avoirdupois weight and to display their beams, scales and weights conspicuously. Bakers had to weigh bread in the presence of the purchaser, even if they sold from bakery carts on the road.

By 1509, there were two bakers' guilds – The Company of White Bakers and The Company of Brown Bakers. They merged in the 17th Century.

Bakers guilds survived through the Middle Ages as the oldest medieval town guilds. Their incorporation did not lighten their burdens. Their property was that of the guild. Their children had to follow the trade and marry within it. Life of both millers and bakers was painful, a condition long true in many other places besides the continent.

PUNITIVE MEASURES

Ancient Persian bakers who short weighted bread or adulterated it with straw did so on the pain of ending in their own ovens. Early London bakers for their infractions endured the humiliation of being displayed in stocks or being pulled through the streets on a cart with bread or whetstones hung around their necks.

For the first infractions, they paid fines immediately on detection. For continuing offenses, officials threw them on the mercy of the public. Often as not, the people devised degrading punishments. Bribery of officials by bakers was common.

BLACKGUARDS AND VILLAINS

Because bread was the ordinary man's chief food for ages, its history has been blackened by unscrupulous cheats. Emperor Justinian reaped a fortune by having loaves short weighted and filled with ashes. As late as the 18th Century, bakers in Constantinople were hanged for cause. This peril led master bakers to hire stand-ins against the day they might be haled into court. Let someone else, they said, be nailed by his ears to the door of our shops if authorities come to arrest us.

Until recent times, bakers in Austria who flouted laws governing bread sales were fined, imprisoned and even beaten.

In general, the baker nevertheless continued to be a man of standing, as he had been in Roman

times. At one time, the murderer of a baker could expect to be fined three times more than one who murdered an ordinary man. And Louis XI of France decreed that bakers should not stand as sentinels for fear they would use that as an excuse for baking a bad product.

THE BAKER CHANGES MORE THAN THE BREAD

While techniques had not progressed much beyond those of Egyptian times – bread molds looked much the same and so did kneading tables – other conditions were beginning to change. Journeyman bakers, after serving apprenticeships, roamed about from three to five years in foreign lands. On their return they had to wait for a master baker to die to find a vacancy. When that occurred, they provided a banquet for the whole guild and promised to obey town ordinances.

BREAD DEFINED AT LAST

At long last some attempt was made to define bread legally. Parliamentary Acts in 1822 and 1836 defined what could lawfully be sold as bread in England. It had to be "made of flour or meal of wheat, barley, rye, oats, buckwheat, Indian corn, pease, beans, rice or potatoes or any of them, and with any common salt, pure water, eggs, milk, barm, leaven, potato or other yeast, and mixed in such proportions as they shall think fit, and with no other ingredients or matter whatsoever."

TABOOS AND SPIRITED MATTERS

While science expunged the mystery from rising doughs, it did not rob man's most common food of its spirit.

Bread has had its beautiful and mystic moments. There is the Brothers Grimm tale of the woman who lost her child. She bade her darling farewell with little shoes baked from a dough made with the whitest flour.

In German provinces, there was a time when no baker turned his back on an oven for fear of being disrespectful.

The very grains that produced flour have been occasion for ritual harvests among European peasants. Germany and Moravia had their wheat brides – the last to bind a sheaf during harvesting.

Grains had their spirits expressed in animal forms. The last sheaf was fashioned as a cock and

became the Wheatcock, to be borne before a harvest wagon. There were Wheat Cows, Wheat Dogs, Wheat Goats, Wheat Men, Wheat Mothers, Wheat Mares, *ad infinitum.*

CEREMONIAL BREADS

All around the world at many times in history, there have been bread taboos. And bread as sacrament has deep religious meaning.

During pagan Day of Blood rites for Cybele, it was taboo to eat bread or flour. Priests serving as living embodiments of Jupiter were forbidden to touch wheaten flour or leavened bread all during their tenure.

Many Esthonians of the Island of Oesel would not eat bread baked with new corn until they had first bitten iron. This was a charm to break the spell of the spirit in the corn.

In Yorkshire it was long the custom for the clergy to cut the first corn. This was probably because the grain was intended for making communion bread.

There were other moving examples of awe and reverence for the grains that nourish man among the Ainus of Japan who eat millet; rice harvesters on the East Indian Island of Buru and in the Celebes; tribesmen of the Neilgherry Hills of Southern India and the Hindus.

Everywhere around the world, new harvests have been the occasion for prayers, sacrifices and rituals. Frazier's *Golden Bough* describes them as "sacraments of first fruits." Primitive as many of them were, there is in them the elevating thought that gratitude for gifts from the earth runs so deep.

THE BODY OF GOD

Before the conquest of Mexico, the Aztecs practiced eating bread sacramentally. To them it was the body of a god. In May and December, they made a dough image of the appropriate god, broke it into pieces and ate it.

The ceremony was a dazzling affair and on the day of celebration, celebrants ate only bread made of beet seeds, honey and maize. With the arrival of Christian missionaries, they were ready to believe priests could turn consecrated bread into the body of their god.

RESPECTFUL TREATMENT

All peoples have shown great respect for bread. Natives of Morocco remove their shoes when eating bread, which they regard as holy food. Some religious sects in India stand when eating everything except bread. That food requires them to kneel. Sicilians deem it a sacrilege to eat bread with their hats on.

"Everything is food, but bread is the great mother," repeat millions of Hindus from their prayer book.

CHRISTIAN MYSTERIES

From earliest times, bread has played a role in Christian mysteries. Hosts, used in religious rites, were baked only by the clergy or virgins. Prayers accompanied baking, and sacred designs, usually the cross, were pressed into the dough.

Nestorian Christians kneaded history into their bread doughs by adding crumbs from previous bakings of sacramental bread. In this way, they claim that today's bread has in it fragments from the bread of The Last Supper.

In some cultures, to break bread with a family is to make you a blood brother. You enter into the soul of the home.

DETRACTORS, TOO!

Something as good as bread had both problems and detractors. The early French schoolboys literally broke bread when they ate. They were packed off to boarding schools with a six months' supply of bread. They had to beat it with hammers and soak it to make it edible.

And white bread attracted the censure of stern Christians. They frowned upon this status symbol as a shameful luxury and lumped it together with shaving beards as a wicked attempt to improve on God's creations.

NO TRIVIAL MATTER

Bread has always triggered visceral response. In the Middle Ages it was a precious "throw away." It was actually a part of tableware – a tablecloth, a plate, a *trencher*. This use of bread as a plate lasted from the time of Charlemagne right through the beginning of the 17th Century. Rich households passed them on to their servants or to the poor who haunted their doorsteps waiting for them.

Trenchers are variously described. Sometimes they were pieces of stale bread that were soaked with food juices and served at the end of the meal. Sometimes they were made of dough – because there was a lack of linen – to cover the surface on which meat was to be cut. They sopped up all the juices from drippings and from wine. They were about six inches wide and half again as thick. When the guests did not finish the meal with these tidbits, they passed to the paupers at the door.

BREAD AND POLITICIANS

And woe to the politicians who neglected the peoples' bread!

French mothers, carrying babies in their arms, marched on Versailles to demand bread. Cries like theirs brought on the French Revolution.

When in more recent times, the Churchill government issued a White Paper describing a plan to decontrol bread, it discovered how attached the English had become to their subsidized bread. They had eaten it for 12 years and clung to it like an old friend. It was palatable, they said, and what was more, the price was better. So the government acquiesced, continued to subsidize the old national loaf and obliged bakers to supply it on demand.

In 1948, even Stalin had a bread scare. Moscow went virtually breadless when something went wrong with the Soviet system of distribution. People were queuing up 23 abreast in bread lines a block long.

Later, villagers in Perm Province complained to *Pravda,* "We have only one bread store. There is always a line around it. We have to stand and wait because we never know whether there will be fresh bread each day or not." Their competitors, it developed, were cows! Fodder was in short supply and the cows had priority.

A political crisis developed in Chile when the government decreed that millers must produce eight pounds more flour than usual from every 100 pounds of wheat.

"War bread!" shouted outraged housewives when they saw the brown bread. "It tastes terrible! It crumbles. It makes our babies sick."

About 42 per cent of the Chilean's daily intake of calories comes from wheat. To protect its stand on grinding more flour from wheat – and saving $10 million in 1973 – the government fought back. It brought forward doctors who testified that brown bread was better for Chileans.

An interesting postscript to government concern with bread is a story from London. In a speech, Home Secretary Robert Carr announced that having abolished such punishments for capital crimes as beheadings and hangings, Britain was now doing away with bread-and-water diets in its prisons. The announcement came in June, 1973.

BREAD CULTURE

In our own culture, bread is material, bread is a tool. The lack of bread symbolizes a shortage of money. A book facetiously titled *The Bread Game* describes realities of foundation fund raising and provides recipes for raising money for worthy causes.

BREAD IS THE MESSAGE

Members of American Women Already Richly Endowed, opposing equal rights amendments for women, made gifts of homemade bread to influence Ohio legislators. They hoped the bread offerings would eclipse the mere carnations and valentines with which a militant women's group was wooing the same lawmakers.

A Swiss Cabinet opened a weekly meeting with the announcement that a satisfied citizen had sent loaves of home baked bread to thank them for their services to the nation.

A MODERN GIANT

Since shortly after World War II, bread has enjoyed annual civic accolades across the United States. Baking, milling and allied industries participate in "Day of Bread" luncheons in New York, Washington, Dallas, Denver, Minneapolis, Atlanta, Wichita and San Francisco.

These revivals of the ancient practice of celebrating harvests are really to advertise the fact that supplying bread for the American table employs many thousands of citizens. The baking industry ranks among the first ten giants on the business roster in the United States today.

FLOUR ARRANGEMENTS

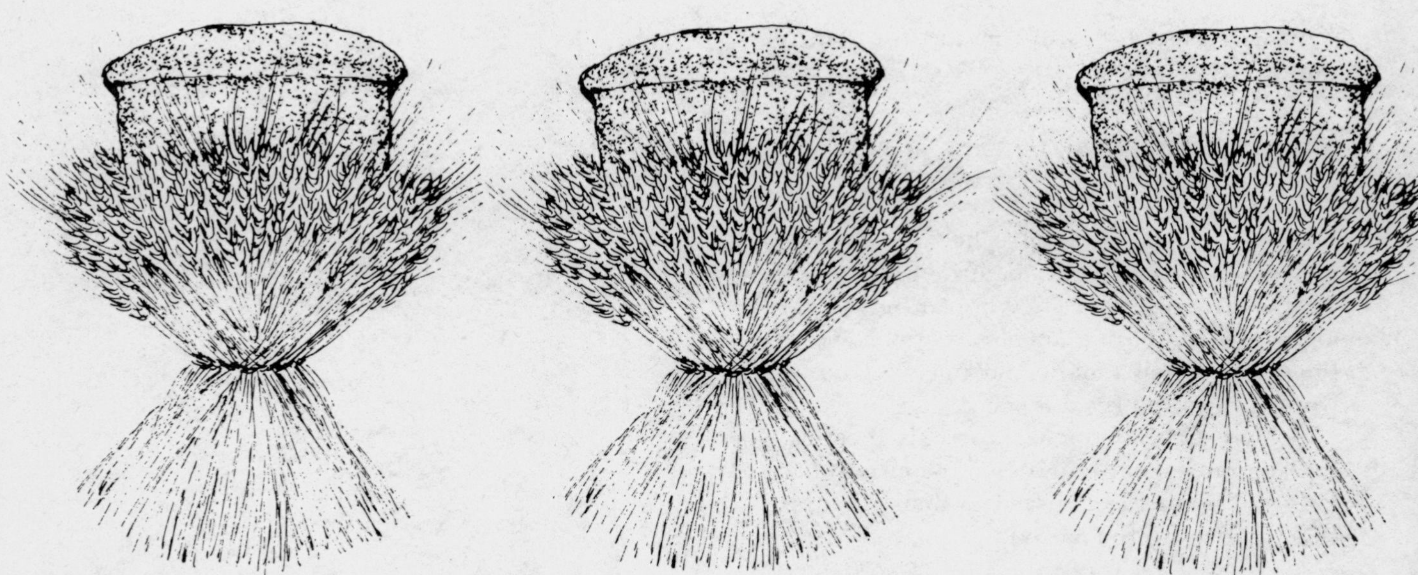

Cereals we take for granted today were exotic and rare in antiquity. Rice was dear and used mainly for medicine. Sorghum appeared briefly in Italy in the 1st Century A.D. Many grains simply were not in demand. Oats were consigned to animal fodder. Millet came forward only in hard times to be used for bread when other grain was unavailable.

Stuff for man's bread came from barley, millet, oats, buckwheat, rice, vetches, beans, peas, lupines, lentils, panic, tree bark and acorns — anything he could lay hands on.

Ruins of prehistoric villages in Northern Italy and Switzerland indicate the acorn was a staple. Plentiful and nourishing, it stored well over the winter and could be ground to flour. The Romans, in fact, depended on acorn bread during wars and famines.

When much later, potatoes were first introduced, there was high hope they would become another bread stuff. They never caught on. The Scottish put potatoes down because they had not been mentioned in the Bible and they were identified with the forbidden fruit of the Garden of Eden. Another telling blow was that they made poor bread.

In classical times, wheat and barley predominated. Barley, like potatoes, lacked acceptance though for different reasons. Normally eaten as a "kneaded thing" not as bread, barley had the low status of fodder for slaves. The special roasting re-

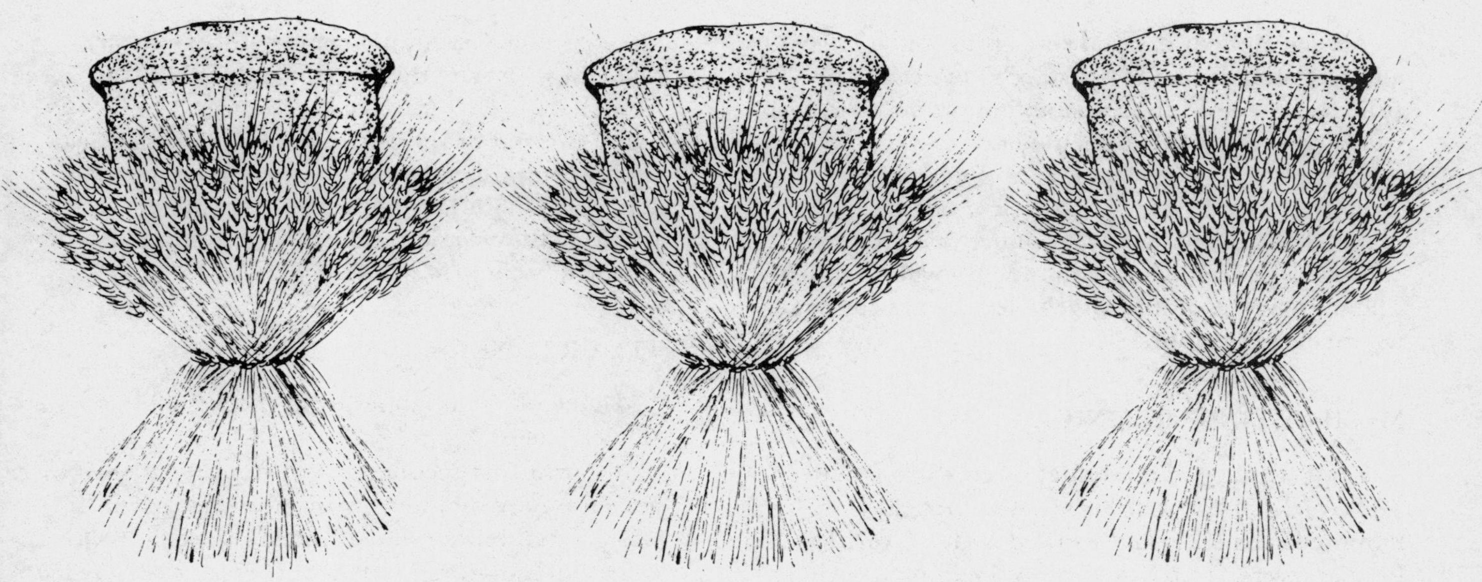

quired to husk barley adversely affected its gluten content and made the flour unsuitable for leavened bread.

EARLY PREFERENCE FOR WHEAT

Bread wheats were important to prehistoric man because he could reduce them more readily to edible form.

The first man to eat wheat may have been an ancient Persian, for bread wheats probably originated there and spread to Europe, China and India.

As a cultivated grain, wheat has been traced in Chinese history to 2700 years B.C. The Bible has many references to wheat growing. It was the chief crop of the ancient Egyptians who revered it enough to bury it with their dead.

Preference for wheat was evident in Greek literature quite early. By the time of Alexander the Great, wheat was the main grain in Greece.

Wheat belongs to the family of grasses, developed by selection and breeding over a period of 5,000 years. More than a thousand known varieties, adapted to almost every climate, exist today.

Cultivated wheats appear in husked and naked varieties. From the latter we make our bread.

All cereal seeds contain some bran and a larger amount of endosperm – a starchy material, the primary source of food and an important source of carbohydrates in the human diet.

Wheat's star component is its gluten. This makes it an ideal bread grain, for flour containing gluten makes a dough capable of trapping yeast-induced carbon dioxide and so encouraging a well risen loaf. The presence of gluten largely determines the baking qualities of flour.

MECHANIZING MILLING

Flour was first the product of crushing stones. The Greeks had a grinding stone device they mounted on a table and worked with a lever. The Romans were the first to invent a complete milling machine in the 2nd Century B.C.

These were big things – the round base being five feet in diameter and one foot high. They were turned by men and later by water wheels. The Romans introduced these water wheels to Britain. The Domesday survey of 1081-86 reported over 5,000 mills in the Midlands and Southern England.

At the end of the 12th Century, the growth of a milling soke made ownership of mills profitable for lords of manors. They monopolized construction and operation and compelled tenants to have their corn ground in the manor mill. To insure this, they forbade the use of hand mills in the home.

By the end of the 18th Century, flour milling was accomplished by steam. Clever engineers followed fast with improvements until millers were boasting they could produce flour completely untouched by human hands.

FLOUR POWER

The word flour comes from the French *fleur* for flower, the best part.

My own first recollection of flour as an entity is graven on my mind in a huge advertising sign. It was painted on the side of Sitek's store on Belknap Street in Superior, Wisconsin. It read: *Gold Medal Flour – Eventually, Why Not Now?*

I saw this question daily as a grade schooler. As it faded with the passing years, I saw it every morning as I made my way to high school. I pondered it and wondered what it meant. I applied it variously to my philosophy of life.

Housewives bought flour in heavy cotton sacks then. These large affairs had replaced the more costly wooden barrels previously used in transporting flour. For a half century few millers sold domestic flour in anything but these standard sacks.

SELL AND SEW SACKS

It was natural that millers would flood the market with "trick" bags to promote flour. In the South, they sold flour in dress print bags from which housewives could make clothing for themselves and their children.

A childhood recollection still fresh in mind was the story my Father told about the usefulness of such flour sacks and their potential for embarrassment. I blushed to hear how a farm mother sewed bloomers for her daughter from flour sacks still bright with the miller's trademark. When the young lady bent over, the whole world could see printed across her bottom, "Mother's Pride." It had been too much trouble to bleach out the trademark with scouring powders, kerosene and bleach.

The same kind of flour sacks inspired Europeans saved from starvation by flour shipped from America following the first World War. You can see a fascinating display of them in the Hoover Institution at Stanford University. They were embroidered – some exquisitely, all sincerely – to thank Relief Administrator Herbert Hoover for his help. All still bear the trademarks, embellished with running threads, wreathed with flowers, messages and intricate stitchery.

No literature on flour has ever so eloquently stated the importance of flour to the human family.

Flours differ from country to country, both in the way they are milled and in the fineness of milling. And flour improves with a little aging.

Many kinds of flour are practically at your finger tips either in supermarkets or in specialty stores. The Glossary and Flour Arrangement Chart below should help you decide what flours you may want to try and how you can use them in bread. Many of these we include in our recipes.

Glossary Of Flours and Bread Stuffs

ACORN FLOUR

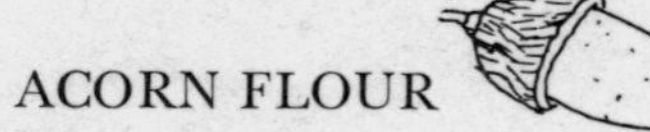

Nut flours are considered easy to digest. Sweet acorns are ground into flour and make a very good bread. Many places in the world nuts take the place of wheat, corn, oats, and barley. Acorn flour has been used for food especially among the North American Indians.

Chestnut flour is also used in bread and once formed a principal article of food in France and Italy.

ALL PURPOSE FLOUR

This is a "family flour" which combines hard and soft wheats. Hard wheat is high in protein and better for bread. Soft wheats are lower in protein and make better biscuits, cakes and pastries. Millers blend the wheats to produce a flour that can be used either for bread or for cakes.

Enrichment Since 1941, millers have enriched whole grain flour with vitamins and nutrients considered essential for nutrition. Laws of 30 states and Puerto Rico require enrichment of flour and bread stuffs. Included are B vitamins, thiamine, niacin, riboflavin and iron.

Bleached vs. Unbleached Flour At one time, it was necessary to store flour in warehouses for months to age and condition it. Aged flour, it was known, produced a better loaf because the gluten became stronger and more elastic as oxygen in the air slightly oxidized the gluten. Since the flour had to be turned to allow air to filter evenly through a batch, results varied with temperature, aeration, and length of storage.

Millers then began to bleach flour to improve color of some grades. They discovered that some bleaching agents matured flour just as though the flour had been stored. So they resorted to chemical bleaching to shorten storage time.

Pure food advocates feel that the use of chemicals this way masks the true flavor and color of flour. They doubt that the addition of chemicals improves baking quality of flour.

Instant or Quick Mixing Flour This free pouring flour instantly mixes in cold liquids while regular flour tends to lump. It sells for more and comes in both all-purpose and cake blends.

Pastry Flour This is a designation for a product that is about one half protein content and one half soft wheat flour. If you squeeze it, it is velvety to the touch and holds its shape. This quality makes it ideal for making cakes and pastries. It is available in both white and whole wheat flours.

Self-Rising Flour This all purpose flour contains salt and leavening – usually bicarbonate of soda and calcium phosphate.

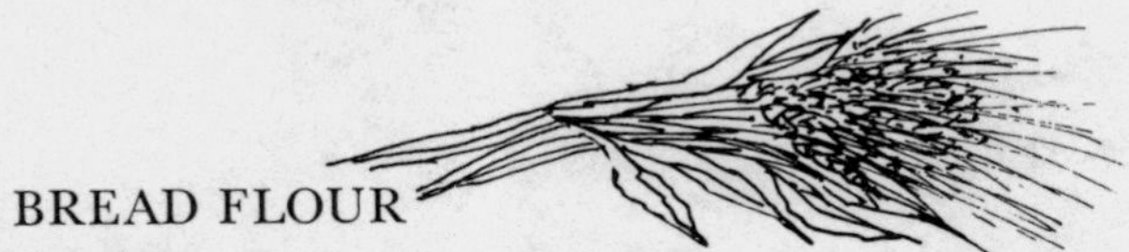

BREAD FLOUR

This is a blend of high protein hard wheat flours. It has just the right amount of gluten to produce high quality bread with fine texture. It is not generally available to the public, being milled especially for commercial bakeries. To get it you have to buy in quantity from a mill.

BARLEY FLOUR

Because it contains no gluten, barley flour is mixed with equal parts of wheat flour to make good bread. A historical grain, it was one of the most ancient of foods. It contains less protein and fewer carbohydrates but more fats and mineral salts than wheat. Bread made with barley has an agreeable flavor. Barley is the source of malt which is barley sprouted and dried. Its chief use is in the manufacture of beer and alcohol.

Barley flakes make attractive finishing decoration for loaves.

BUCKWHEAT FLOUR

Not a cereal, buckwheat was introduced into Europe in the Middle Ages from Manchuria and central Siberia. Its flowers provide bees with honey of a dark color and strong peculiar flavor. The flour is dark and usually an ingredient of griddle cakes. It is used in Europe to make "black bread" and we include it in our recipe for pumpernickel.

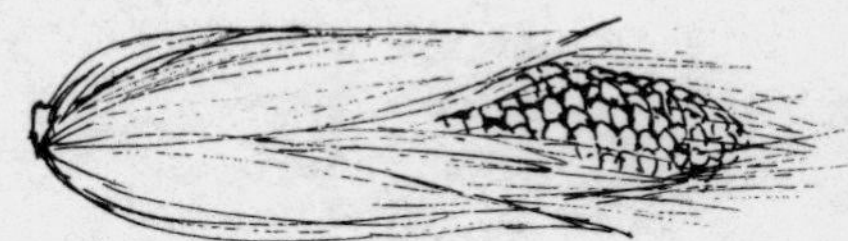

CORN FLOUR

Corn flour is a finely ground flour that can be mixed with other flours to make good bread.

CORN MEAL

Corn meal, sometimes called Indian meal or maize, lacks gluten and is often mixed with all-purpose flour to prevent crumbling in making corn bread.

For all practical purposes yellow or white corn meal is equally nutritious, the color simply depending on the color of corn used. Flavor does differ, however, white corn meal having a nutty flavor.

Water-ground corn meal, specified in recipes is merely corn meal that has been stone ground, the stone grinding having originally been powered by water. We have not found any packages on the market that are specifically labeled "water-ground."

Corn meal is used exclusively in Johnny cake,

pones, and tortillas. In other breads, corn meal is sometimes mixed with equal parts of wheat and rye flour.

COTTONSEED FLOUR

This low fat flour has a protein content five times greater than whole wheat flour. It improves flavor and imparts a dark yellow color. You can blend it with other flour – 1 cup to 6 cups of wheat flour – to increase protein. This product is comparatively new.

GLUTEN FLOUR

Gluten flour is the result of removing a large part of the starch from wheat flour. It is 40% protein, compared with the 12 - 15% contained in other flour. It is useful for diabetics.

It is the gluten in flour that makes bread making possible. It is a protein or mixture of proteins which become stickly when mixed with water. This mass may be blown up with air or any other gas, and it finally sets when baked. If the walls of the cells are not stable enough to stand, when the gas has been expelled by heat, the bread falls or is said to be heavy.

GRAHAM FLOUR

Dr. Sylvester Graham, an American vegetarian in the early 1800's first recommended this flour. It contains all of the wheat berry. The inner part of the kernel is ground to uniform mass while bran layers are left flaky and coarse.

Your grandmother probably made Graham bread with a potato sponge because she thought that this was the way to keep it fresh and sweet longer. And she made the brown bread because everybody allowed that it was good for you!

MILLET FLOUR

This flour makes a nutritious, palatable bread. It darkens soon and crumbles easily. It can replace 1 to 3 cups of other flour. At one time millet fed half the inhabitants of the earth. In some areas it is still used the way rice is used.

OAT FLOUR

This product is finely ground from groats – the untreated, natural hulled oats. It is blended with other flours for baking bread.

Oats seem to have been the original grain plant of Europe where it has been known for 2,000 years. It is always cultivated. It has never been discovered growing in the wild. Oats in the form of meal and groats – rolled, cut or gritted – are used for breakfast cereals. Cooked oatmeal makes an excellent addition to bread doughs, both for nutrition and taste. Use 1 cup of the cereal to 3 cups of wheat flour.

POTATO FLOUR

This dense, compact flour must be blended with other flour or dry ingredients in mixing bread dough. It produces a moist, slow-staling loaf.

RICE FLOUR

Rice flour is ground from broken, imperfect grains, During World War I, rice flour was widely used in the United States as a substitute for part of the wheat flour in making bread. It proved very satisfactory, replacing up to 30% of other flours.

Flour is made from both white and brown rice. Brown rice flour can be substituted for wheat flour if you are allergic to wheat, or blended with other flours to add texture. The rice bran, produced from outer layers of the brown rice kernel, can be added to other flours like wheat germ.

RYE FLOUR

Rye, like wheat, contains gluten. The gluten in rye is stickier. This characteristic makes it an excellent medium for yeast growth. Rye bread is darker and less porous than wheat bread. Rye flour is often mixed with wheat in making bread, the optimum proportion being two parts of wheat to one of rye. Small quantities of rye flour may be added to wheat flour to assist fermentation because of its high proportion of soluble protein.

Rye gives bread a special aroma and somewhat sour taste. You can now buy a pumpernickel type rye meal which has the consistency of corn meal.

SOY FLOUR

Soy flour, made from toasted soybeans and having a slightly sweet, nutty taste, is preferred by some to soy flour made with the raw beans. Soy beans contain more concentrated food elements than any other common food. This includes most known vitamins and all the essential amino acids.

Soy's protein content is a high 40 - 45%. It is 15 times richer in calcium and 10 times richer in iron than regular wheat flour. For these reasons, soy flour is an important nutritional addition to other flours. You can substitute up to one part of soy flour to five parts of wheat. Some cooks use more — as much as one part to three of wheat.

Soy flour tends to cause heavy browning of bread crust. Lacking gluten, it cannot be used alone in yeast breads. We like to use it also in cookie, pancake and muffin recipes.

WHOLE WHEAT FLOUR

This product contains all of the wheat kernel, including the bran and the germ, reduced to flour consistency. Used alone it produces a heavy flat loaf. Used with unbleached white, it makes a bread of good character.

OTHER BREAD STUFFS

Today's demand for highly nutritive blends has brought on a mixture of flours and exotics both creative and extreme. We have sampled many breads up and down the West Coast from California to British Columbia, rejoicing in quite a number and being amazed by a few. The claim for all of them was that they are good for people!

WAR BREAD PRECEDENT

One doesn't normally think of war shortages as having any saving graces, yet such shortages of wheat during World War I happily made mixing of wheat with oats, rye, corn flour, barley and rice a necessity in making bread.

Excellent bread was made with the addition of 25% of these other flours to wheat. Prior to that, the replacement of 3% of other flours, nuts and cereals had been an allowable standard.

SCRIPTURAL BREAD

Contemporary searchers for bread that makes good food have excellent antecedents. Two ladies, we understand, have been teaching a seminar in Connecticut on "The Bible Has The Recipe." They cite the very rugged Ezekiel Bread found in Ezekiel 4:9:

> Take thou . . . unto thee wheat, and barley, and beans, and lentiles, and millet and fitches, and put them in one vessel, and make thee bread thereof.

Fitches in recent editions of the Bible are translated "spelt" and it is also thought they may refer to fennel.

The first loaf the ladies made was very heavy!

FOR HEALTH'S SAKE!

There are many potential bread stuffs on the market – often found in health food stores and in special departments of supermarkets – that add nutrition, distinctive taste and interesting textures to everyday breads.

These include sea weed; hulled sunflower seeds; seeds of wheat, barley, millet, rice, alfalfa and mung beans for sprouting; and flours made with green peas, lima beans and garbanzos. Cereals you cook for breakfast – oatmeal, farina and multi-grain products – also make fine additions to bread doughs.

It is in this seeking out of ingredients – trying a little at first, then a little more until you have balanced them in your own recipe – that you have the option of inventing your own loaf.

KEEPING THE LID ON BREAD STUFFS

As with gunpowder, you keep your flour dry. Flour stored at about 13% moisture content and free from insect pests will remain sound from six to eight years! Maintaining nutritive values and qualities of flour even for a short term storage imposes definite conditions.

FLOURS, GRAINS, CEREALS AND DRY SKIM MILK

Store these at room temperature in containers you can close tightly enough to keep out moisture, dust, and insects. Clean glass jars with screw lids and rubber seals make excellent containers as do empty coffee cans with tight, plastic covers.

We use a quick drying pen to write contents right on plastic lids. This becomes especially important when you are trying out all sorts of exotic flours, cereals and other bread stuffs. Don't try to remember which is which. If you buy packaged goods, you can paste the label right on the storage container.

BAKING POWDER

Keep a tight lid on and store in dry place. Baking powder is good only in proportion to the amount of gas that is liberated when the powder is moistened. If you think your supply has become inactive, put a teaspoon of it in hot water. If it bubbles vigorously, it is all right.

WHEAT GERM

The high fat content in this product makes it advisable to store under refrigeration. Keep in a screw top glass container.

YEAST

We use dry, granular yeast because of its superior keeping qualities and buy it by the pound. Once the package is opened, we store the yeast in the refrigerator in a tightly capped glass jar. It keeps for months.

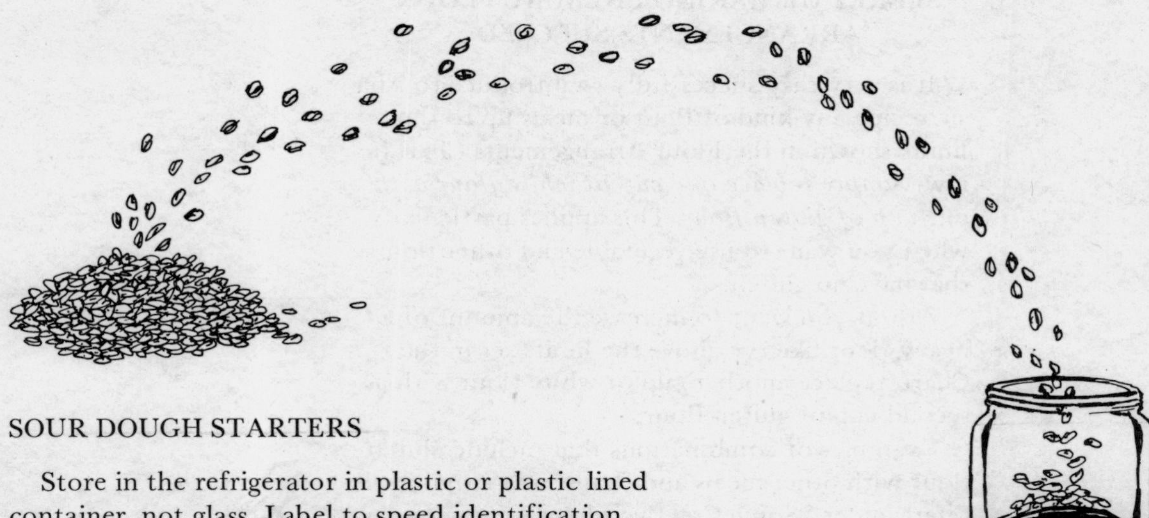

SOUR DOUGH STARTERS

Store in the refrigerator in plastic or plastic lined container, not glass. Label to speed identification. If you have not used the starter at least twice during a month and refreshed it with additional flour and water, add ½ teaspoon of sugar. Your starter is all right even if a semi-clear liquid forms on top. Just stir back into the mix.

GRAIN AND SEED SPROUTS

Health food stores sell screen-topped jars with tight lids for sprouting seeds and storing them. The jars with lids screwed tightly and placed in the refrigerator will keep sprouts in sound condition until you are ready to use them.

CHARTING THE COURSE

Our FLOUR ARRANGEMENTS CHART makes it easy to determine how much flour or exotic stuff you can introduce to bread without upsetting its balance or overwhelming its taste and texture, or lessening its keeping quality.

Keep in mind that introducing a super nutritious ingredient does not mean that if a small amount is good, a larger quantity is necessarily better. The Cornell Formula, for instance, is the result of careful research. Although it calls for minimal amounts of soy flour, dry skim milk and wheat germ, it does improve nutritional values of bread.

There is nothing to say you can't introduce more of anything if you want to, of course. Just be prepared to have a bread that may embody characteristics you don't expect and can't predict. It can "fall." It can be almost uncuttable and crumble on the bread board. It can be very heavy and tough. If these possibilities don't bother you, go ahead!

In all our recipes, we use only unbleached flour, stone ground products, and products free from adulterants. None of the breads we bake last long enough to excuse spoilage retardants. Anyway, we have found no breads we can't freeze if we want to make extra loaves.

SECRET OF MAKING UNUSUAL FLOUR ARRANGEMENTS SUCCEED

It is very easy successfully to introduce to a basic recipe any kind of flour or meals up to the limits shown in the Flour Arrangements Chart below. *Simply replace one cup of white flour with one cup of gluten flour.* This applies particularly when you want to use vegetable and other flours that have no gluten.

Also if you want to increase the amount of a heavy flour like rye above the limits set in the Chart, replace another cup of white flour with a second cup of gluten flour.

Examples of combinations that include gluten flour with other meals and flours are starred in the Chart under "Some Creative Flour Arrangements."

Flour Arrangements Chart

This Chart is a guide showing how much of various flours and bread stuffs you can substitute for equivalent amounts of unbleached white flour to create a new bread. It is based on a 6-cup, 2-loaf white bread recipe.

Example: If you use 1 cup of acorn flour, you will use only 5 cups of white flour called for in the recipe.

Flours, Seeds And Meal You Can Substitute For White Flour	*Substitute This Amount For An Equal Amount Of White Flour* CUPS	TABLESPOONS
Acorn flour	1	
Barley flour	3	
flakes, cooked	1	

Some Creative Flour Arrangements

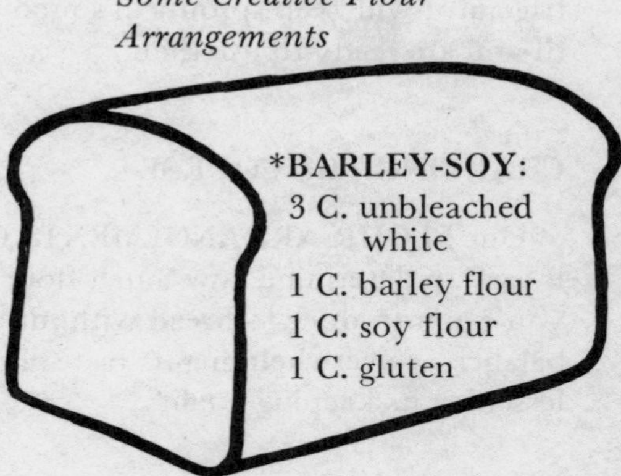

**Gluten flour in these creative flour arrangements insures that dough will rise evenly and develop desirable texture and volume.*

Flours, Seeds And Meal You Can Substitute For White Flour	*Substitute This Amount For An Equal Amount Of White Flour* CUPS	TABLESPOONS
Bran flour	1	
flakes	2	
Brewers' yeast		2-4
Buckwheat flour	1½	
Carob powder	2	
Chia seeds		2
meal		2
Coconut flour	½	
Cooked cereals	1-2	
Farina		
Oatmeal		
4-Grain		
7-Grain		
Corn flour	2	
meal	1	
Cottonseed flour	1	
Cracked Wheat		3-4
Flaxseed meal cooked	½	
Garbanzo flour (chickpea)	1-2	
Gluten flour	4	
Graham flour	4+	
Lima Bean flour	1	
Matzo flour	1	
Millet flour	2	
meal, cooked	2	

Some Creative Flour Arrangements

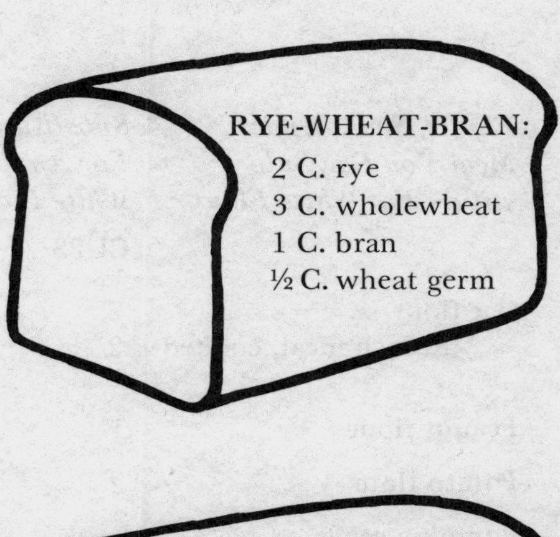

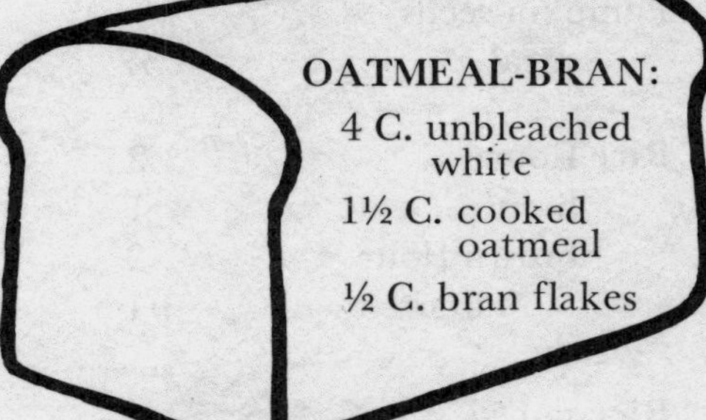

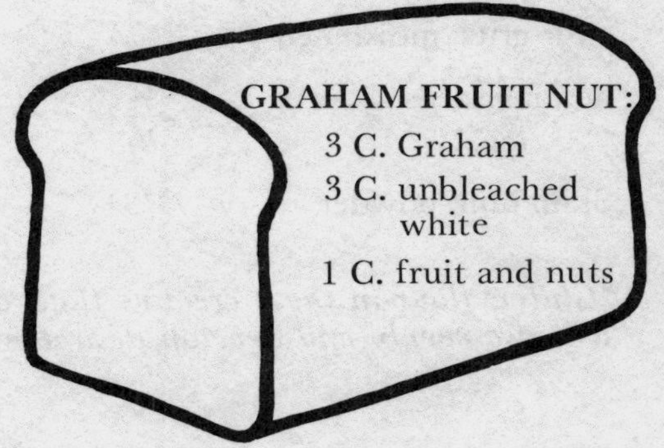

Flours, Seeds And Meal You Can Substitute For White Flour	*Substitute This Amount For An Equal Amount Of White Flour*	
	CUPS	**TABLESPOONS**
Oat flour	2	
Scotch meal, cooked	2	
Peanut flour	1	
Potato flour	2	
Pumpkin seeds		2-4
meal	½	
Rice flour	2	
bran	1	
brown flour	2	
bran	1	
Rice polish	1	
Rye flour	2	
meal	2	
grits, moistened		3-4
Sesame seeds	½	
meal	½	
Skim Milk powder	1/3+	

**Gluten flour in these creative flour arrangements insures that dough will rise evenly and develop desirable texture and volume.*

Some Creative Flour Arrangements

CRACKED WHEAT-OAT-HONEY:

¾ C. cooked cracked wheat
½ C. softened steel cut oats
1 C. whole wheat
3 C. unbleached white

RYE-CORN MEAL:

3 C. unbleached white
2 C. rye
1 C. corn flour or meal

***MILLET-GLUTEN:**

2 C. millet flour
½ C. gluten
3 C. unbleached white
1 C. dry skim milk

Flours, Seeds And Meal You Can Substitute For White Flour	*Substitute This Amount For An Equal Amount Of White Flour*	
	CUPS	**TABLESPOONS**
Soy flour	2	
meal	2	
grits, moistened	½	
Sunflower seeds	1	
meal	1-2	
Urid flour	1-2	
Water Chestnut flour	1	
Whole wheat flour	6	
bran	1	
flakes	1	
Wheat Germ	1	
Wheat Germ flour	1	
Wheat Grits	1-2	

Some Creative Flour Arrangements

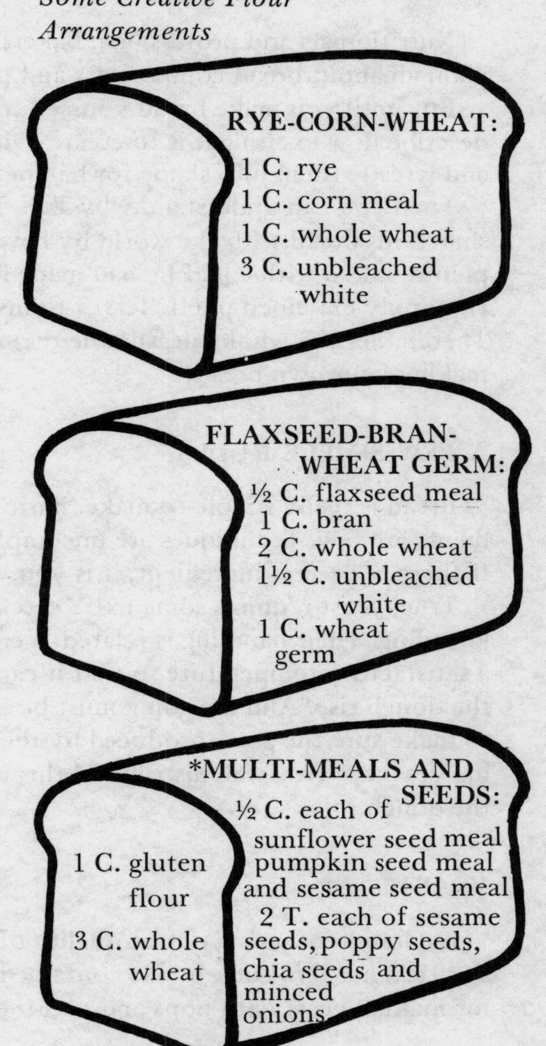

**Gluten flour in these creative flour arrangements insures that dough will rise evenly and develop desirable texture and volume.*

THE WAY BREAD IS MADE

A VERY PERSONAL EXPERIENCE

Nutritionists and professional bakers can explain all about bread components and processes.

But until you make bread yourself, no one can describe how exciting it is to create living doughs and wrestle them into shape for baking.

Then you can understand why T. S. Eliot shared his bread with the world by having his picture taken with a loaf he had made himself. He simply extended poetic fervor to his kitchen. Therein lies the whole pleasurable reason for making your own bread.

A FEW SIMPLE RULES

Bread is really simple to make. Basic ingredients are few. Techniques are uncomplicated. If there is a secret ingredient, it is you.

True, yeast requires some extra care as does kneading. Their handling is related. Yeast wants a satisfactory temperature so that it can make the dough rise. And kneading must be adequate to make sure the gases produced by the fermenting yeast are very well distributed throughout the dough.

YEAST

In Grandmother's day, the quality of yeast was a critical matter. Cook books contained recipes for making yeast with hops and potatoes. The result was a starter that had to be regularly renewed. The quality of yeast is still critical.

In our recipes we use granular yeast because it is convenient to use and keeps well in storage.

In making bread, you can use one tablespoon of yeast for each three cups of flour or cup of liquid. When you use the maximum amount of yeast, you can shorten the proofing cycle. This simply means, it takes less time to make the bread. Keeping this in mind, you can make bread from start to finish in two and one-half hours.

KNEADING

From Roman times, men have invented an astonishing number of outlandish mechanical devices just to duplicate the unique action of human hands in kneading bread.

And a famous French baker in 1778 thought it was worth the trouble to define kneading. This was the mixing, he said, of yeast, flour, water and air to yield a new substance with special properties. Because of it, dough became soft, flexible and homogeneous.

Kneading is a chemical process. It allows carbon dioxide gas, developed during fermentation, to escape. If allowed to remain in the dough, the gas checks the fermentation power of the yeast. Kneading brings the yeast into closer contact with the dough, stretching it to accommodate all the tiny gas bubbles. Baking sets this porosity.

SOME TIPS

Kneading dough for the first time is something like diving for the first time. Plunge right in. Your initial anxiety will quickly turn to ebullient confidence in a single session.

When we are making bread, we use a large, heavy pottery bowl because it stays warm and holds still during mixing. We warm the bowl and other utensils in hot water and towel them. Then we measure out the maximum amount of flour called for in the recipe.

We stir flour into the liquids a cup at a time with a wooden spoon, sweeping in a wide arc around the bowl until the flour disappears. We keep adding flour, stirring and beating until the dough begins to ball and leave the sides of the bowl.

This is the moment. Nothing stands between you and the dough now.

GET SET!

Wash your hands, clean your fingernails and roll up your sleeves. Flour your bread board, making a circle of it larger than your ball of dough. Turn the dough out of the bowl on to this little carpet of flour. Work fast. The dough will start to spread out. Keep pushing it back into the flour, sweeping a bit over the edge and top of the dough. You will be ready to knead when the dough has absorbed enough additional flour, has stopped spreading so fast and is no longer too sticky to handle.

PUSH, PULL AND ROLL!

Kneading involves shoving the dough away from you with light, pushing, downward strokes of the heels of your hands and pulling it back.

Probably no two people knead alike. So don't worry if you don't duplicate a picture you have seen in a book. Remember, there was a time when bakers chose to knead with their feet! You are doing the right thing so long as you are working the dough; pushing it hard and pulling back; folding it to a square shape when it begins to stretch out like a big sausage; and finally ending with a good ball of dough that is smooth and elastic to the touch.

MAKE IT BEHAVE

The important thing is to be thorough. The whole idea is to make certain that all the gas bubbles developed during yeast fermentation are very well distributed.

During kneading, you may discover you need more flour to keep going. Add a little at a time.

How long does all this take? Some bakers say 300 strokes. Others suggest kneading dough 8 to 10 minutes – even more.

With experience, you will develop a lovely rapport with dough. You will know exactly how long to knead, simply by the feel of the dough in your hands.

THE WHOLE BEAUTIFUL BUSINESS

Let's get on with the whole loaf and go through the six steps of breadcrafting with the how's and why's.

Here's a recipe that looked so easy years ago that a non-cook memorialized it by copying it for her kitchen file.

GRACE GRIMES' HOME MADE WHITE BREAD

1 tablespoon yeast	2 tablespoons sugar
¼ cup warm water	2 teaspoons salt
2 cups scalded milk	6 cups warm, sifted flour
2 tablespoons shortening	

In Six Easy Steps

1. ASSEMBLE and MEASURE

To make every minute count, start by putting yeast in warm water. It will take about 10 minutes to foam. While yeast is working, assemble ingredients and utensils.

Fill large mixing bowl with warm water to take the chill off.

Get out your measuring cups, wooden spoon, sifter, sauce pan and bread pans.

BREADCRAFTER'S TIPS AND HINTS

Yeast. Since sugar feeds yeast, bakers often use part of sugar in recipe to "start" yeast.

Yeast and water. Water is best medium for dissolving dry yeast. So milk is not used for this.

Warm mixing bowl. Just about every good cook works with warm bowls and utensils in making bread.

2.

SCALD MILK,

COOL AND

ADD YEAST

BREADCRAFTER'S TIPS AND HINTS

Pour 2 cups of milk into sauce pan. Add butter (or other shortening), sugar and salt. Turn on heat.

Milk gives bread a softer, thinner texture and adds protein and calcium. Bread made with water has a thick, crisp crust.

Butter, oil or margarine are more or less equal substitutes. Fat flavors bread and helps keep it moist.

Sugar and salt add flavor. The more sugar, the browner the crust. Too much sugar and not enough shortening will toughen the crust.

Sift 6 cups flour onto a piece of waxed paper or paper plate. Hold extra flour handy for kneading and dusting bread board.

Flour. Always measure out full amount called for in recipe. Amount used will vary from day to day, depending on type of flour, amount of gluten, temperature and humidity. Don't be afraid to use more flour than recipe calls for.

Milk is now warm. Advance heat to bring milk just below boiling to scald it. Remove from burner and cool.

Scalding. This occurs when milk is just below boiling point. Tiny bubbles appear around edge of pan, and surface wrinkles.

Empty warm water from mixing bowl and wipe dry. Spoon sifted flour lightly into measuring cup and level off. Put 4 accurately measured cups of flour into bowl. When yeast has foamed and milk is lukewarm, combine mixtures.

Fresh milk is scalded to prevent development of sour flavors. Milk makes bread an almost complete food, contributes flavor, adds color to crust. Bread also keeps better.

Yeast develops flavor, adds nutrition and supplies vitamins.

BREADCRAFTER'S TIPS AND HINTS

3. MIX DOUGH

Pour combined liquids over flour and mix with wooden spoon or electric mixer, adding 2 more cups flour, 1 cup at a time, until dough begins to stick together and starts to come away from sides of bowl.

Flours. Different flours absorb liquids differently. If recipe calls for sticky flours like graham, rye, gluten or buckwheat, start with 2-3 cups and add rest when dough is ready to knead.

Mixing. Mix thoroughly if you want to avoid lumps and streaks in bread. You can blend most of the flour with a mixer. The more you beat the dough, the finer the texture of the bread.

4. KNEAD

Sprinkle half a cup of flour on bread board over an area slightly larger than ball of dough. Scrape dough out of bowl onto floured board. The dough will start to spread. Work quickly, scooping flour up over dough until you have a manageable ball.

Start kneading with floured hands, adding flour to board until dough stops sticking and is as smooth and soft to the touch as the back of a baby's neck.

Kneading. Can you knead too much? Not really. You will tire before the dough does! Kneading should be fun. A friend compared kneading to raising weights in a gym. He was working too hard!

Kneading time varies. You soon get the feel. When the dough is not sticky, but smooth and satiny, it is ready.

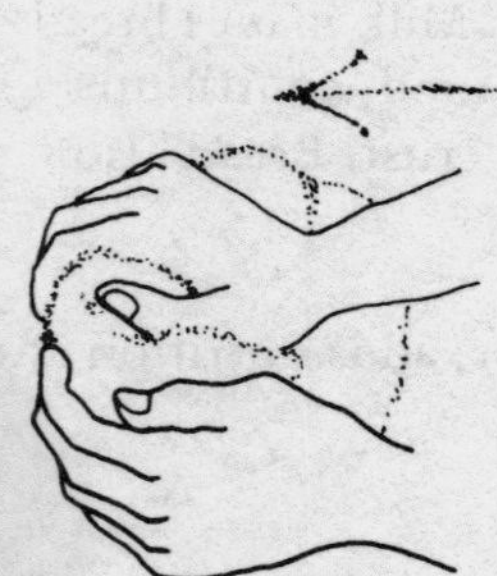

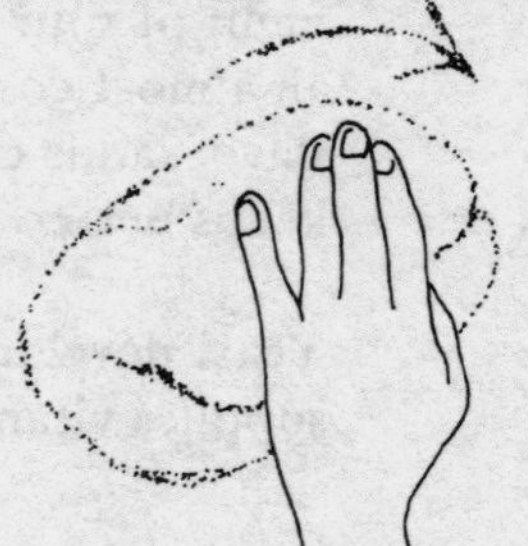

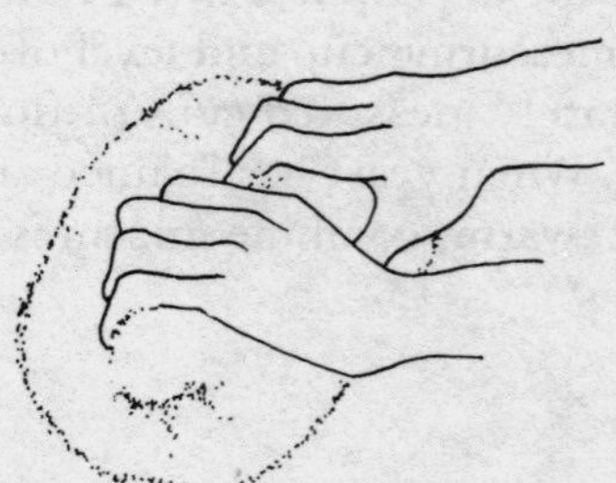

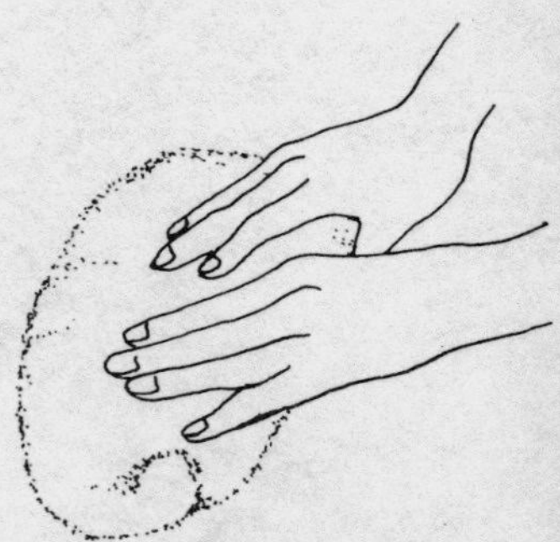

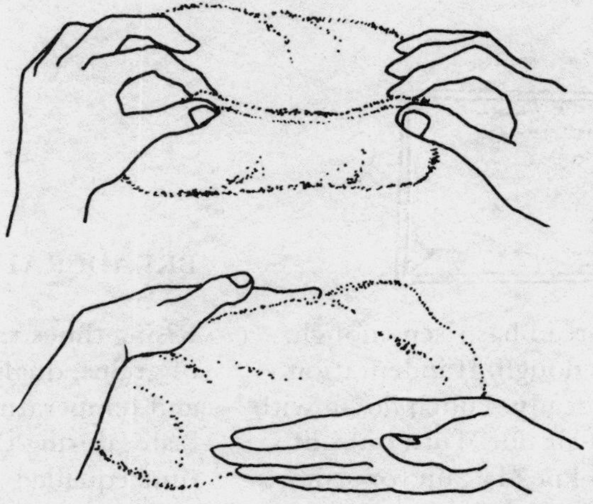

5.

LET RISE

Place kneaded dough in buttered bowl, cover with towel, lid or plastic wrap. Let rise in a warm place until double in bulk, usually an hour.

Some good places to set bread to rise are:

An oven with pilot light; or warmed for 1 minute at 200°; or with bowl of warm water on lower rack.

In a sink filled with warm water and refilled as water cools.

On a gas stove near pilot light.

On a radio, if not too hot and radio is left on to provide constant heat.

Some NO-NO's: Do not put bowl on a radiator or in direct sunlight or over a hot air vent. Such heat can kill yeast.

BREADCRAFTER'S TIPS AND HINTS

Keep it warm and cozy. Rising should be neither too fast nor too slow. Cold slows action of yeast (and sometimes this is a useful technique). Steady warmth is best–85° – 90°.

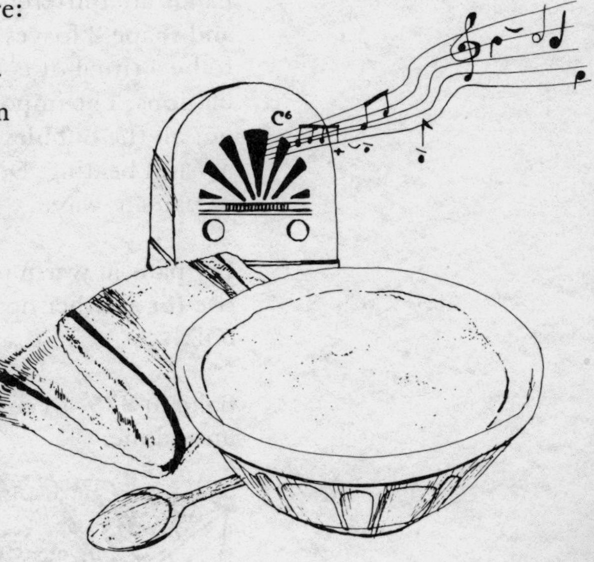

6.

SHAPE AND BAKE

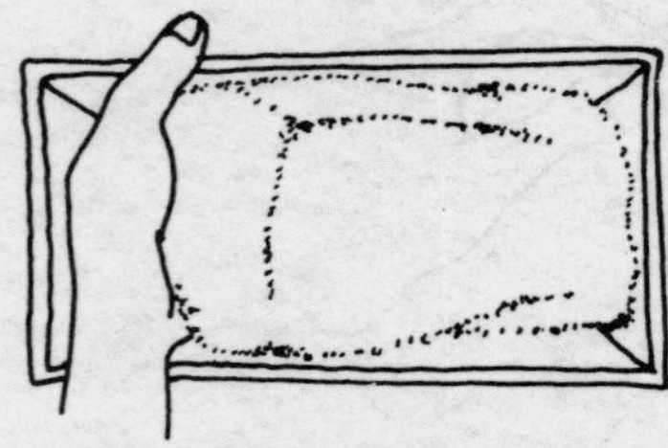

When you think bread has risen enough, press a finger into dough. If indentation remains, dough is ready. Punch down with your fist to get all air out. Turn out onto floured board and knead again for a short while to assure a fine, close texture of finished bread.

Butter 2 bread pans thoroughly. While hands are buttered, divide dough in half and shape 2 loaves. This does not have to be a ritual of correct folds and manipulations. The important thing is to work out all the bubbles, stretching and pulling and beating. Dough will take shape of pan anyway.

Put pans in warm place and let dough rise for another hour or until double in bulk.

Bake in 375° oven for 35-45 minutes or until done.

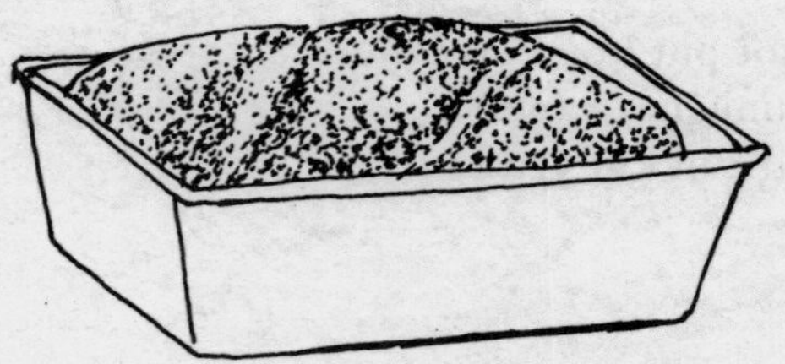

BREADCRAFTER'S TIPS AND HINTS

Rising times vary, depending on heaviness of grains, quality and amount of yeast, and temperature of kitchen. Bread rises faster during the day – 4 hours of day time equalled 12 at night according to an old rule of thumb.

Holes in bread develop when dough has not been punched down or kneaded sufficiently.

Butter the crust. If you like a good brown crust, brush finished loaves with melted butter or margarine.

Variety of shapes. There are many ways to shape loaves and decorate them. See Chapter V, "On Experimenting With Breads and Bread Stuffs."

Second rising. Texture and grain of bread becomes coarse if temperature is too high. Watch this.

When is bread done? When bread is brown and shrinks slightly from sides of pan, it is done. You can also turn bread out of pan and thump it on the bottom. If bread sounds hollow, it is ready. If not, don't hesitate to return it to the pan and bake a little longer.

BREADCRAFTER'S TIPS AND HINTS

COOLING

Always cool finished loaves on a wire rack. This lets air circulate around the whole bread so the carbon dioxide and other gases can leak out. Otherwise, you end up with a soggy crust.

When bread is completely cool, you can wrap it, store it or freeze it.

Control cooling. Crust may crack if loaves are cooled too fast or left in a draft. This affects keeping quality.

STORING

There are two ways to keep bread fresh. The best method is to freeze it. Advantages are that bread slices easily with a sharp knife; toasts beautifully without thawing; makes good sandwiches to take to work or on picnics. The cold keeps the sandwich filling fresh until lunch time.

The second way to keep bread fresh is to keep it in a metal box at room temperature. Keep breadbox clean and dry to prevent bread mold. For odorless cleaning, wash the box with baking soda in the water, not soap. Pioneer women wrapped bread in clean towels and stored the bread in crocks.

How to store bread. Wrap bread in waxed paper or plastic to prevent absorption of moisture and foreign flavors from other foods. We double-wrap breads, first using waxed paper and then storing in a plastic bag.

Breadcrafters' Flow Chart

EFFICIENCY EXPERTS ANALYZE TIME AND MOTION

The Breadcrafters' Flow Chart is a time-and-job analysis of the two-loaf Grace Grimes White Bread Recipe. The most helpful feature of the chart, from an efficiency man's point of view, is the way it highlights with a heavy line what is called the *critical path.*

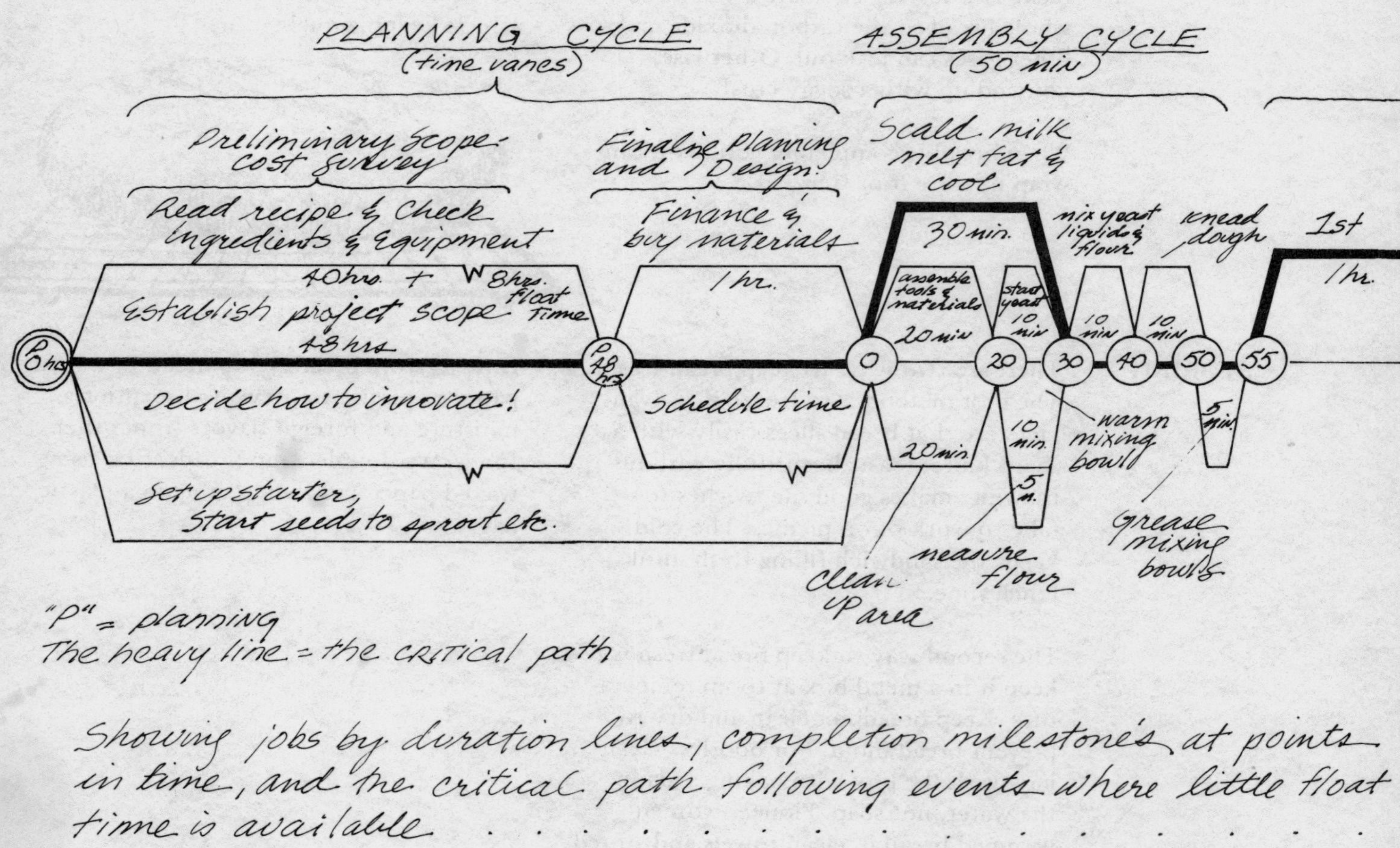

The critical path traces those operations that take the longest time for you to complete during each cycle of breadcrafting. It shows you which jobs you must start first or cause delays in everything else you do.

While the chart suggests a 48-hour, pre-baking Planning Cycle, you may be ready to bake this very minute. If so, fine! Five hours and ten minutes from now, you can be ready to cut, eat, freeze and evaluate the bread. Other recipes take more or less time to complete. But once you are acquainted with critical path operations, baking efficiently will be a snap.

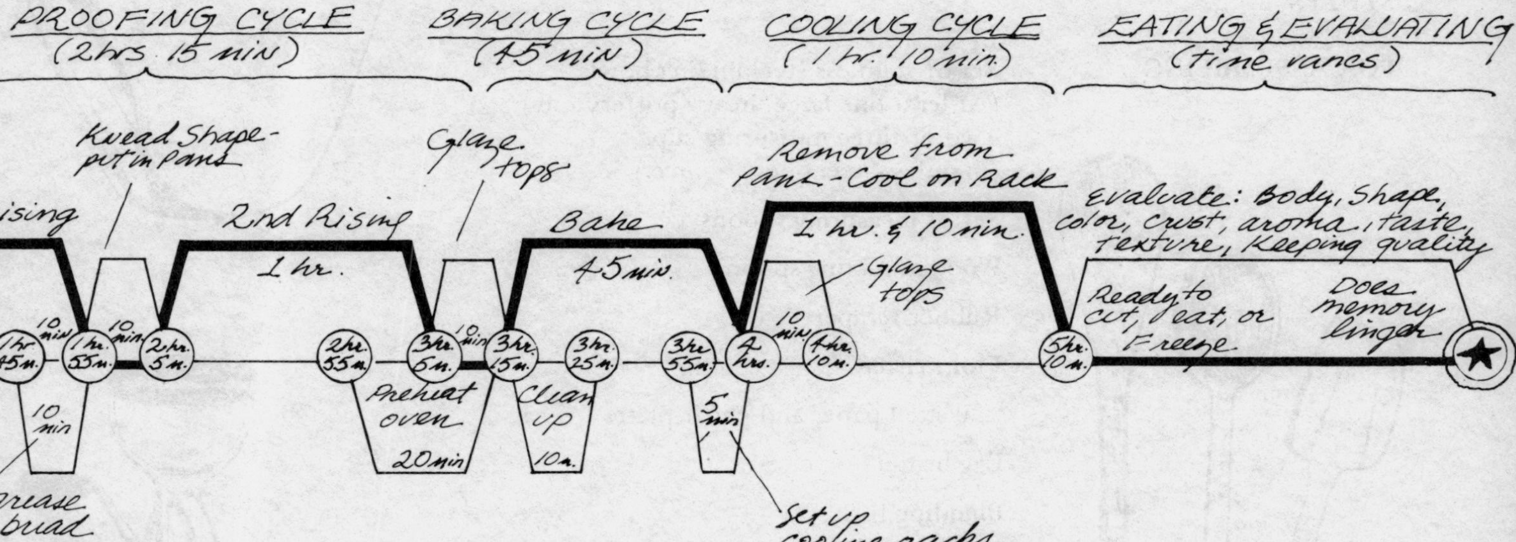

= EVENT CIRCLES: they mark "stop" or "start" at point in time, w/ total elapsed time in HRS. & minutes.

. . to assist in analyzing, scheduling and managing the process of breadcrafting.

Equipment We Have Found Useful

FOR BULK STORAGE	Flour and sugar cannisters
FOR MILLING FLOUR AND PREPARING BREAD STUFFS	Flour mill, food grinder, grater
FOR ASSEMBLING	Set of stainless steel mixing bowls (At least one large, heavy pottery one) Two or three measuring cups (Stainless steel ones are nice.) Set of measuring spoons Wooden mixing spoon Rubber scraper Flour sifter Waxed paper and paper plates Egg beater Blending fork Bread board Rolling pin Pastry brushes Biscuit cutter
	OPTIONAL: Electric mixer; bread maker Pastry cloth

FOR BAKING	Bread pans — rectangular Cake pans — round and square Casseroles Cookie sheets and pans Muffin tins and Brioche pans Aluminum foil
	OPTIONAL: Impeccable house plant sprayer to spray breads just before removing from oven. Great crust crisper! Also cast iron bread pans, for crusty loaves.
FOR COOLING	Wire racks
FOR STORING	Waxed paper Plastic freezer bags Breadbox

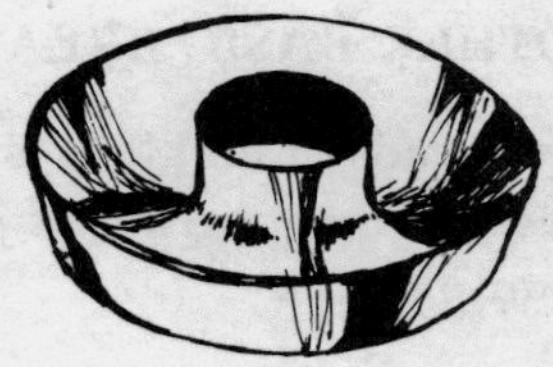

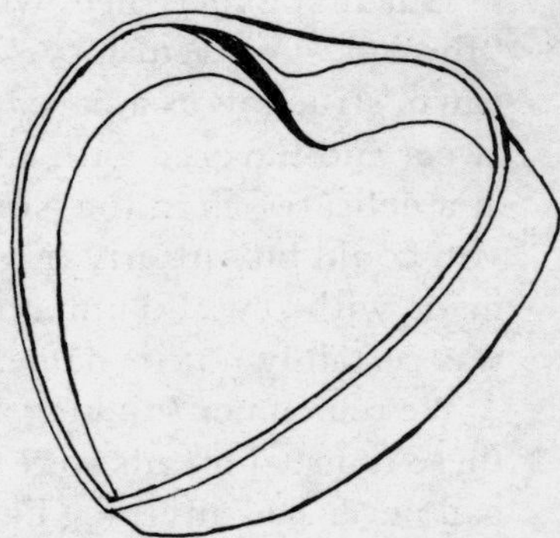

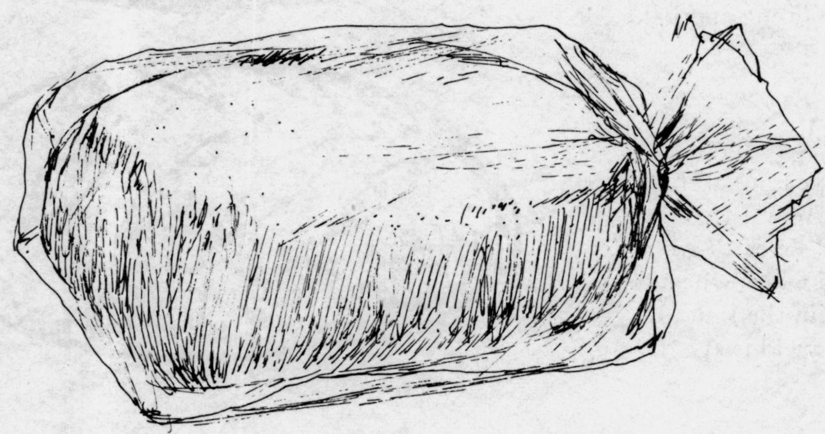

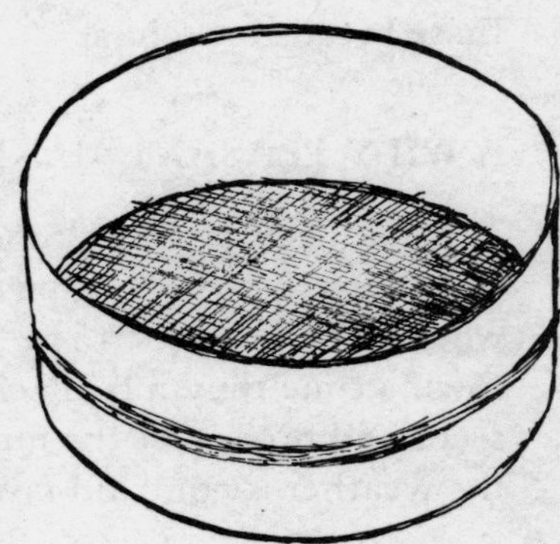

OTHER BASIC BREADS TO MAKE

Breads of all kinds are yours to make. Rye and whole wheat breads as just as basic as Mrs. Grimes' white bread.

RYE HAS BEEN DESEGREGATED!

Our first experiences with rye bread were "foreign." A Swedish rye, made by Swedes in our town, struck us as a party bread because it was sweet and flavored with anise or cardamom. And at a delicatessen in the North End of our town, you could buy utterly fragrant salami sandwiches made with Jewish Pumpernickel Rye, though that was certainly not its name.

We remember thinking at an early age that these unusual breads were so good, how come we had never had anything like them before? Where had they been all our lives? It never occurred to us then – as it does now – to go home and bake these breads ourselves.

A WILY PEASANT MANEUVER

It has been said that Siberian peasants refuse to believe that rye is a species different from wheat. They call their rye "black wheat." At sowing time they mix black with white wheat seeds and broadcast the mixture in the field. If the weather is cold and raw, the yield is rye. If

the weather is mild and warm, the harvest is wheat. Either way, the combination wins.

Like the clever peasants, breadcraftsmen mix wheat and rye, too. If they use rye flour alone, they get loaves with poor cell structure. Products baked with 100% rye are never as light and porous as products that contain wheat flour. And that is why most recipes for rye bread also contain wheat. Its gluten content makes good cell structure possible.

WHEN YOU MAKE RYE BREAD . . .

Keep two things in mind when you make rye bread. Rising time for rye bread is usually longer than that for white bread. Your control of proofing temperature at 80° – 85° is important.

Also, whenever milk is used – whether sweet, sour or buttermilk – it should be scalded to obtain the best grain and texture in the finished bread. Then make sure it is lukewarm before you add to yeast mixtures. Commercial sour milk, cream and buttermilk curdle when scalded, but this does not affect the finished product.

Here are two excellent recipes, one using thick sour milk and the other calling for potato water. The first is from the family archives. The second is a contribution from a friend, Max Anderson.

SOUR MILK RYE BREAD

½ teaspoon sugar
1 tablespoon yeast
¼ cup lukewarm water
2 cups boiling water, cooled a little
2 cups light rye flour
2 cups white flour sifted
½ cup brown sugar
2 teaspoons salt
1 cup thick sour milk, scalded and cooled
1 tablespoon margarine
2 tablespoons molasses
White flour to make a stiff dough

Dissolve yeast and sugar in ¼ cup warm water. Pour 2 cups of hot water into warm mixing bowl and stir in rye flour, the 2 cups of white and the yeast mix. Beat well until you have a smooth batter. Set bowl to rise in a warm place for at least an hour.

Stir into yeast batter the brown sugar, salt, sour milk, margarine, molasses and enough flour to make a stiff dough. Turn dough out on lightly floured board and knead until smooth and elastic – about 10 – 12 minutes. Place in buttered bowl, turning to butter top of dough, cover and let rise another hour until light and almost double in bulk.

Punch down. Divide dough in half and shape into 2 loaves – round for baking casseroles or oblong for regular bread pans. Butter baking pans and let dough rise again in warm place. Bake at 375° for 30 – 35 minutes or until done. If you think loaves are browning too fast, cover with sheet of aluminum and continue baking.

Remove loaves from pans and cool on wire racks. While loaves are still warm, brush crusts with a mixture of hot water and molasses or dark corn syrup. This makes for a nice sweet crust and a shiny, lacquered look.

Yield: 2 loaves

FANCY FOOD FROM A FOOD FANCIER

Max Anderson operates a quality grocery in the Hawthorne Hills area of Northeast Seattle. Busy as he is all week long, he delights in baking rye bread for his family for Sunday breakfast.

When he became interested in bread baking, he first researched the subject, reading all he could find on bread in the public library. He wanted to know about flours, yeast, and the special gift potato water had to make to his family's Old World Rye Bread recipe.

We knew he was interested in perfection when he said, "I get better flavor by crushing cardamom seeds myself instead of using commercially ground ones." And he is a practical man: he uses aluminum pie tins on which to bake his bread.

MAX'S POTATO RYE BREAD

3 cups warm potato water
1 tablespoon yeast dissolved in
1/4 cup of the potato water
1/3 cup molasses
1/2 cup white sugar
1 tablespoon salt
1 tablespoon freshly ground cardamom or anise seed
1/4 cup shortening
1 cup rye flour
Enough white flour to make kneadable dough

As Max observed, "I don't have to tell you how to do it." He did add that milk may be substituted for potato water, oil for shortening. He mixes the bread, he kneads it, he lets it rise until double in bulk, he shapes round loaves, and he bakes them on pie tins at 375° for approximately 35 minutes.

Yield: 3 loaves

EAST-TO-DO WHOLE WHEAT BREAD

Use stone ground wheat and unbleached flour in this recipe and feel terribly healthy!

WHOLE WHEAT BREAD

1 cup milk scalded
1 tablespoon salt
¼ cup honey
¼ cup shortening

1 cup lukewarm water
2 tablespoons yeast
3 cups whole wheat flour
3 – 4 cups white flour

Combine milk, salt, honey and shortening and stir until smooth. Add water. When mixture is lukewarm, add yeast, then whole wheat and beat for about 2 minutes. Beat in enough remaining flour to make a kneadable dough. Turn out on bread board and knead about 10 minutes. Place kneaded dough in buttered bowl, cover and let rise in warm place until almost double in bulk, about 1 hour. Punch down, divide dough in two, shape into loaves and place in well-buttered pans. Cover and let rise again until almost double in bulk and bake at 375° for 50 minutes. Decrease heat to 350° and bake another 30 minutes.

Yield: 2 loaves

AND HOW ABOUT SOME GLUTEN BREAD?

Gluten flour is expensive. It is usually a helpmeet to other flours that are low in gluten. The following recipe gives you a very high protein, low starch bread that is reminiscent of the taste of shredded wheat. It also has a lot of bounce.

GLUTEN BREAD

Prepare a batter with

1 tablespoon yeast foamed in 1 cup lukewarm water
2 tablespoons sugar
2 cups milk scalded and cooled to lukewarm
1/3 cup soy flour
2 tablespoons wheat germ
2 cups unsifted gluten flour

Cover and set to rise in warm place for 1 hour. Punch down hard and stir in

3 cups of gluten flour mixed with
1 teaspoon salt

Knead until springy and shape into loaves. Put in well buttered loaf pans and set to rise in warm place for another 30 minutes. Start baking at 400° and after 5 minutes, reduce heat to 375° and bake for about 30 minutes or until done.

Yield: 2 loaves and
4 hamburger buns

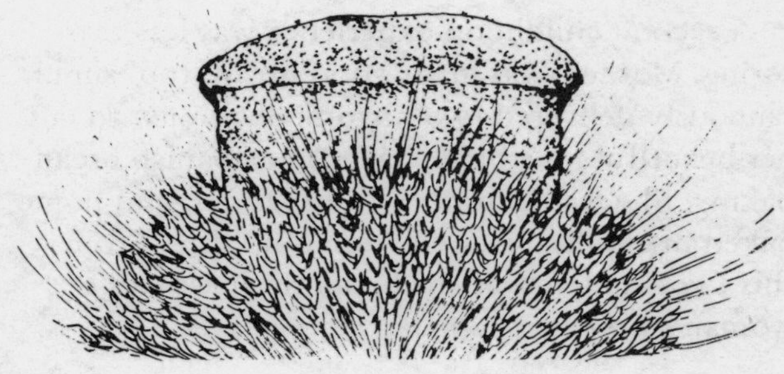

TRACING BREAD LINES

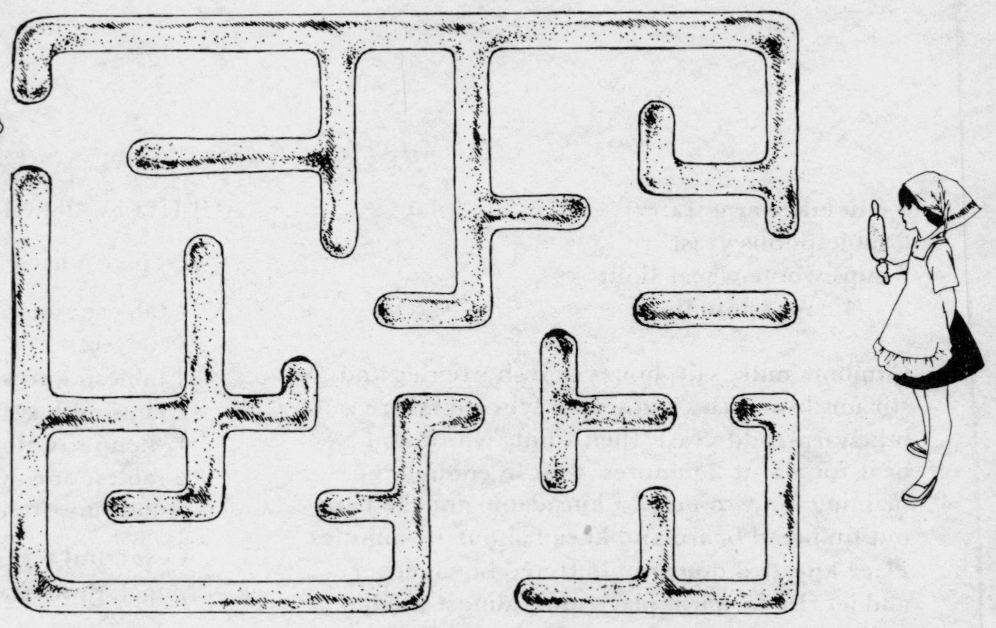

My personal history of bread at its lavish best began in the summers of childhood on my Grandmother's farm.

Just for me, Grandmother would shear a golden crust from the top of a whole snowy loaf still warm from the oven. On it she spread thick cream skimmed off the top of a milk pail that hung in the pump well. She topped it with a sprinkling of brown sugar. It was good!

A second childhood experience was less reassuring. Mother who made good bread, too, simultaneously delivered two historic decisions: to cut her beautiful long black hair and to banish bread baking. She was in tune with the times, and home baked bread disappeared from our table. From this I concluded that the bread business was a woman's burden.

A third circumstance did not improve my attitude.

A KILLING COSTUME

Domestic science texts of two generations ago prescribed how to address oneself to the art of baking. The young cook donned a white uniform. Buttoned to the belt was a white huck hand towel, a white flannel-filled holder for retrieving hot pans from the oven; and a blue percale bag, the use of which was never explained.

Put on a large and clean apron, begins one prissy recipe. Roll up your sleeves above the elbows. Tie something over your head lest hair fall. Take care that your hands are clean and have a basin of water and a clean towel handy

Do not make trouble for others by scattering materials and soiling the table or floor, or by the needless use of many dishes. And do not stir with your hands! Use a wooden spoon, especially in summer.

I loathed a bibbed apron and headband I had to make in a sewing class. Pure white, ugly and impossible to keep spotless, they were put together under the sour eye of a virago. Needle pricks drew little drops of blood here and there. The outfit had no romance and less style.

That costume killed baking for me.

ROMANCE TO THE RESCUE

It never occurred to me then that bread making would ever become important. When I married, however, The Man fancied he had married an old fashioned girl who naturally could bake bread.

I was eager to please. Unfortunately at the time, I confused baking readiness with literacy. I could read: therefore, I could bake bread. Rye bread was nice. So I would start my bread career with the first rye bread recipe I could find in my three cook books.

Every detail of that small kitchen in Larkspur, California, is still sharp. I wasn't wearing the prescribed costume, but I was up to my elbows in goo. I gurgled with helpless rage as I tried to extricate my hands from dripping strings of dough.

To no one in particular – I was alone – I yelled, "No silly bread dough is going to tell me what to do!"

With that I attacked the sponge and made it behave. By the time I had the bread in the oven, I fiercely resolved that my bread-loving man would help me eat the disaster.

To my glad surprise, it was lovely stuff! Praise crowned the struggle. No bread since has cowed me or my husband. We have concluded that bread – like many growing things – will come into being and flourish, even when the maker is awkward and amateurish.

ABSOLUTELY ANYONE CAN MAKE THIS BREAD

Admittedly, the trauma of the rye cooled my ardor for awhile. Not until my husband found a simple, no-knead recipe for French bread – the Village Bakery closed about the same time – did I take up the art in earnest.

That French bread recipe we included in our annual Christmas letter one year. Good reports have followed it through the years.

You can succeed with it and even go on to experiment with variations on the theme. It goes all together in one big mixing bowl.

ONE BOWL, NO-KNEAD FRENCH BREAD

Dissolve 1 tablespoon yeast in 1 cup lukewarm water. Add this to 4 cups unbleached flour sifted with 1 tablespoon sugar and 2 teaspoons salt. Add just enough of a second cup of lukewarm water to stir up a soft, sticky dough.

Let rise in a warm place until double in bulk – about an hour and a half. When dough is high, punch it down vigorously and divide into 2 loaves.

Pop into very well buttered pyrex casseroles, about 3 inches deep and 6 inches in diameter. Let rise again until double in size. Place in a cold oven and set heat at 350° and bake an hour.

Yield: 2 loaves

This simple recipe with its five ingredients plus tap water led to many experiments. As we grew bolder, we added eggs and seasonings and spices and extracts and herbs. We mixed flours – white and whole wheat and rye. We added orange and lemon rind and glacé fruit and leftover coffee.

Everything delighted us, except for one experiment. We added too much wheat germ to one dough and it responded by practically blowing up in the oven. The result was that we learned to try a little before we went overboard on any changes in a bread recipe.

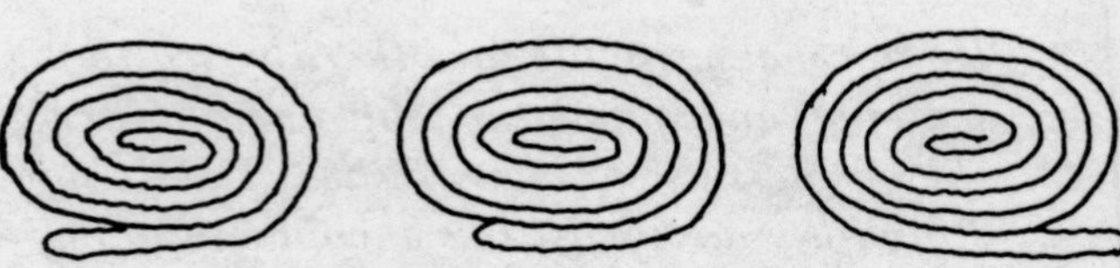

Some Historic Breads

For a long time, now, we have found it exciting to investigate the staff of life and its place in the story of man – to trace its lineage and bake our way through history.

AN ANTIQUE FRENCH BREAD

The technique for making this bread is reminiscent of that which produced the old Roman delicacy, Parthian bread. It, too, was set to rise in water before kneading and baking. Like many revived arts, this one requires some dedication, leisure and not a little energy at well spaced intervals. The heavenly crust alone is worth the trouble.

PARTHIAN STYLE FRENCH BREAD

Rise early and mix 1 tablespoon yeast and ½ cup lukewarm water with enough flour – about 3 cups – to make a dough. Knead well. Roll into a ball, cut a cross on top and drop into a bowl containing 2 cups lukewarm water. Set in a warm place until sponge is light – about 1½ hours.

Next, add 5 or 6 cups unbleached flour with 1 teaspoon salt and 1 tablespoon melted shortening. Knead for 20 minutes. Place in warm bowl, cover and let rise in a warm place free from draft. When dough is light, punch down vigorously. Let rise again. Repeat this process several times.

Form into long rolls and turn onto buttered pans. Let rise in a warm place. When very light, dust with flour lightly, slash tops of loaves diagonally at intervals with sharp knife and bake at 350° for about 50 minutes.

When bread is nearly done, brush with diluted and slightly beaten egg white. Just before taking from the oven, sprinkle with water and close oven to crisp crust for a minute or two. We use our impeccable "dahlia sprayer" to sprinkle the loaves in this final operation. It works like a charm. So you might add a house plant sprayer to your bread making equipment!

Yield: 2 large loaves or
3 modest size ones

AN OLD EGYPTIAN BREAD TRICK

Another way to make French bread was new thousands of years ago. It requires a starter, the magic formula for which the ancient Egyptians evolved. These days, you can buy a small package of starter clipped to a folder of instructions on how to make sour dough French bread. Or you can just as easily make the starter yourself.

SOUR DOUGH STARTER

Mix 2½ cups flour with 1 tablespoon yeast and enough lukewarm water to make a thick batter. Keep in a warm place, uncovered, for 24 hours or until it has a yeasty smell. It is ready to use. Store under refrigeration, but bring to room temperature before you use it in the recipe that follows.

Note: When you dip into the starter for a recipe, replace an equal amount of flour mixed with warm water to the consistency of the original starter.

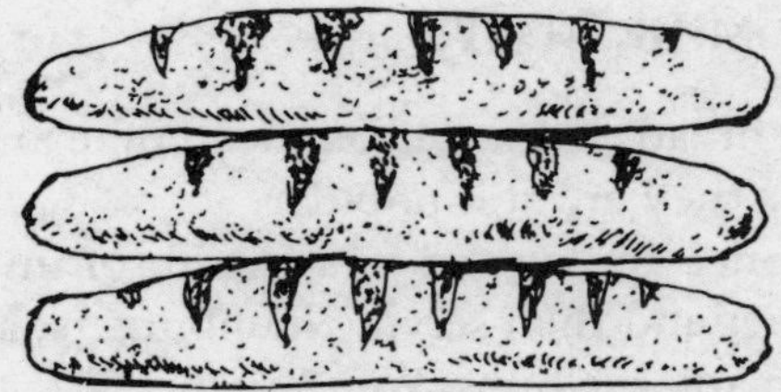

SOUR DOUGH FRENCH BREAD

In a large bowl, dissolve 1 tablespoon yeast in 1½ cups warm water. Add 1 cup starter and stir well. Add 4 cups unbleached flour, 2 teaspoons sugar and 2 teaspoons salt. Mix well. If you use your electric mixer for this operation, set at medium speed.

Cover and let rise in a warm place until double in bulk – about 1 hour. Next add 1 cup flour in which you have mixed ½ teaspoon soda. Knead until smooth, about 10 minutes.

Set to rise again in a warm place for another hour. When double in bulk, form 2 or 3 round loaves and place on well buttered baking sheet sprinkled with fine corn meal. Allow to rise until double in bulk. Just before putting in the oven, slash tops of loaves as for tick-tack-toe. Place a small pan of hot water in the oven and bake breads about 35 – 40 minutes at 400°.

Yield: 2 big or 3 modest loaves

MAKE MINE FLAT!

Flat breads are as old as they come and it is no wonder they are still popular.

We once apologized to a friend for inviting him to dinner and then serving hamburgers, albeit on home-made rye buns. We thought, of course, that he would be making comparisons with times we prepared Chinese banquets and birthday parties for which we went all out.

"Well," he said, "one of the meals I enjoyed most was the one at which you served those Arabian flat breads."

"Why that meal?" we exclaimed.

AN AMERICAN RIJSTAFEL

"Because I had never eaten flat bread before," he said, adding, "and it was the biggest hamburger bun I had ever seen. It was the size of my plate and when I split it open, it made such a neat container. You had so many things to put in it. It was fun making selections. It was as if you had invented an American Rijstafel," he concluded.

We had provided all kinds of fillers, relishes and condiments, salad greens and chopped raw vegetables – everything we could think of. But we had underestimated the measure of delight the do-it-yourself participation would provide.

A BREAD SPOON IN ITS NATIVE SETTING

Selma Ekrem recalls how Arabian nomads celebrated a religious holiday with feasting. An enormous platter arrived with roasted lamb atop a mound of rice cooked with pine nuts and raisins. Before each guest were hunks of flat bread. No silverware or plates were anywhere. The hostess demonstrated how to proceed. Using a piece of flat bread like a spoon, she scooped up a slice of lamb and some rice and brought them to her mouth without spilling a grain of rice. The meal ended with rosewater poured over everyone's oily fingers.

ARABIAN FLAT BREAD

Dissolve 1 tablespoon yeast in 1¼ cups lukewarm water. Add 3 cups flour mixed with 2 teaspoons salt. Stir into a rough ball and knead until smooth. Add more flour if necessary. Set to rise in a warm place for about 1 hour.

Divide dough into 6 balls and knead until round. Flatten with a rolling pin until you have a cake about ¼ inch thick and 5 inches in diameter. Set to rise for 45 minutes on an ungreased baking pan.

Bake in hot oven about 15 minutes. When done, they will be brown and puffed up. This creates the pocket you can slit open for the fillings.

Yield: 6 breads

Note: You can make these with both unbleached white and with whole wheat flours. Try using 1 cup of whole wheat to 2 of white.

The flat bread freezes very well. The texture is decidedly crunchy; the taste, very satisfying.

THE NORWEGIANS HAVE A WORD FOR IT, TOO

Although I had a Norwegian Grandmother who spoke with a soft, swinging accent, I knew little about things Norwegian until I taught English in a small Wisconsin high school. The territory was Norwegian and a standing joke starred a traveling salesman.

Encountering lefse for the first time, it is said, he spread it on his lap as a napkin.

Cognoscenti knew better. They spread the limp flat bread with butter, sometimes sprinkled it with sugar and cinnamon, rolled it up and enjoyed.

Lefse was baked on the top of wood burning stoves. Its appearance on the tables of the local restaurant was selective and regarded as a special compliment. One had to appreciate lefse to merit it. We understand that this Norwegian favorite is available in the gourmet section of Woolworth's in San Francisco, and that patrons like it as an extra with a cup of coffee or tea. It is not usually served with meals.

LEFSE

Mix well together 6 cups cooled, riced potatoes, 1 tablespoon melted butter, 1 cup flour and 1½ teaspoons salt.

Roll large spoonfuls of dough in your hands until you have round shapes. Flatten and roll very thin on a well floured board. Norwegians use a special lefse rolling pin but you can get

the same effect by pricking the rolled dough with a fork.

Bake individually on a grill or electric frying pan at medium heat. Lefse is done when you have baked both sides and small brown spots appear.

A NORWEGIAN FRIEND REMEMBERS LEFSE

Customs about serving lefse vary. A friend recalls how lefse came to table warm at suppertime. "The pattern of the lids on the wood stove was baked right on the cakes. They were about 12 inches in diameter. First we spread them with butter and sprinkled sugar on them. Then we folded them in half and rolled them up so that we could hold them in our hands and the butter wouldn't run out. We held them like bananas as we ate them.

"Another way was to fold lefse in half once and then in half a second time so that you had a triangular piece like a flat open cone. That kept the butter from pouring out, too.

"We kids ate lefse any time it was available and was nice and warm. That made the butter melt. Probably some people put jam on lefse but we never did."

ANOTHER NORWEGIAN FLAT BREAD

Quite different from lefse is a flat bread that is round and hard and baked on a grill or on a cookie sheet in the oven. In small villages in the mountains of Hardangerfjord, Norwegian housewives bake them in stone ovens.

NORWEGIAN FLAT BREAD

Combine 1½ cups sweet milk, ½ cup butter melted and cooled, and 1½ cups whole wheat flour sifted with 1 teaspoon baking powder, ½ teaspoon soda and 1 teaspoon salt.

Roll out paper thin on a floured board. Bake on a grill or electric frying pan or bake in a quick oven on a baking sheet.

AND A LOW BOW TO CHINESE PANCAKES

Peking pancakes represent a very venerable place in bread history. They are really small, pale, tasty and marvelously flexible flat breads. They receive sauces and solids alike without becoming soaked or unwieldy. They roll up without breaking or falling apart. They can be handled neatly without spilling. They are the all-purpose food wrap.

Around them you can build a whole meal by folding in meats, eggs, sea foods, chicken and condiments. They are traditionally included in the first course of Peking Duck and serve as wrappers for the duck skin along with sauces and little spring onions.

PEKING PANCAKES

Mix well in a heavy bowl 1 3/4 cups flour and 2/3 cup boiling water poured in gradually.

Knead this dough until it is smooth and elastic – about 5 minutes – and you have a lump the size of a soft ball. Pull it out into a uniform roll about 18 inches long and cut off 1-inch pieces.

Dip one piece in sesame oil and press onto an unoiled piece. Roll out both together with a rolling pin to make a very thin 4-inch cake. Fry in oiled wok or heavy skillet at moderate heat until bubbles form. Turn and fry other side. Repeat until all dough is used.

As you remove each cake from the skillet, pull apart to make two cakes and stack them under a damp towel. When all cakes are ready to serve, steam them for ten minutes to reheat.

ANCIENT AND HONORABLE BAO

To eat Chinese steamed bread is to eat ancient history. It has been food from time immemorial for all those artists whose exquisite work fills the Oriental collections of the Walker Gallery, Seattle Museum, the De Young and the Fogg and many others. And even today, it won't pay you to try to improve on this recipe if you are entertaining a Chinese friend!

FERMENTED STEAMED BREAD

2½ cups flour
4 tablespoons sugar
2 tablespoons salad oil

1 teaspoon yeast
1 cup warm water

Dissolve yeast in lukewarm water. In a bowl, mix well with flour, sugar and oil. Knead. Return to bowl and cover with damp towel or cheese cloth and set to rise in warm place for 2½ to 3 hours.

When dough has risen to double in size, add a little flour and knead again thoroughly. Roll dough into a long roll and cut into 2-inch lengths. Shape into buns. Place in a warm spot for 15 minutes and allow to rise again. Steam for 15 minutes. Allow water in steamer to come to boil before setting in buns. Serve hot.

Yield: 12 buns

THE BREAD THAT LAUNCHED A SCORE OF RECIPES

Another tasty, historical product is Salt Rising Bread. In these rushed times, you can rarely have it unless you make it yourself.

Pursuit of its mysteries has been frustrating and challenging at the same time. We came to know the bread when trips through the countryside led past a bakery that advertised, at infrequent intervals, "Salt Rising Bread, Today Only."

The sign might just as well have read, "One Time Only," for the bread soon passed into history.

Sadly enough, we had developed a taste for it before we understood its rarity on the market. No help for it but to try to make it ourselves.

We started to collect recipes that originated in China and extended all the way to Old Virginie. Recipes came from old cook books, newspapers and magazines. Some were very long and detailed. Others were maddeningly unrevealing. One was the product of a woman who swore she had had 18 years experience with salt rising bread and "mine is No. 1."

Another self styled expert said it was the kind of vessel you used that made the difference, and various recipes start out, "In a pitcher or other deep vessel, make a sponge..."

One cook recommended fruit jars that could be covered and set in a pan of hot water. Another recommended a big sugar bowl or a new tin dipper. And most early salt rising bread recipes were accomplished with the help of wood burning stoves – something we didn't have.

IT'S THE BACTERIA, NOT THE BOWL

The facts are that corn meal, potatoes, flour, milk and other ingredients contain certain bacteria that are salt tolerant. They can be encouraged to grow and multiply in a temperature that would kill yeast.

These gas-forming bacteria do for salt rising bread what yeast does for other breads. The gas produced is about 2/3 hydrogen and 1/3 carbon dioxide.

The loss of materials, due to decomposition and volatilization of some of the constituents of the flour is much less in salt rising bread. It has a fine grained texture and an utterly tantalizing fragrance as it bakes.

No matter what recipe you use, plan to keep an eye on this dough for 24 hours or more.

Two recipes follow – one very old and the other from an American pioneer cook book.

CHINESE MAN T'OU – STEAMED BREAD

Mix a rice bowl of flour with enough water to make a soft dough. Keep in a warm place for a day or two until sponge has begun to rise and has a sour odor.

Add water and 4 or 5 bowls of flour. Put this in a warm place over night or longer if necessary. When this has risen well, dissolve enough baking soda in water to counteract the acid in the sponge, and add. Knead dough thoroughly and shape into buns. Steam. Small buns should be

steamed 15 – 20 minutes; larger ones, a half hour.

Always reserve part of the dough for starting buns next time you steam buns.

PIONEER SALT RISING BREAD

In a warm bowl, mix 3 cups warm milk, 1 teaspoon each of salt and soda, 2 tablespoons corn meal, and enough flour to make a loose batter. Cover and set in a warm, draft-free place for 6 or 7 hours or over night, until mixture starts bubbling.

We use a covered bean pot and place it in a plastic picnic chest with a 15-watt light bulb and a portable thermometer. This arrangement achieves a steady temperature of 110° – 115°.

When batter bubbles, add 2 cups of flour and enough boiling water to make a smooth, elastic dough, working it for about 30 minutes.

Let rise until very light and add more flour – 3 or more cups – until dough is stiff enough to knead. Knead for 10 – 15 minutes. Form 2 loaves, place in buttered pans, cover and let rise until more than doubled.

Bake in moderate oven, 375° for 10 minutes, then at 350° for 25-30 minutes longer.

Yield: 2 rather flat loaves

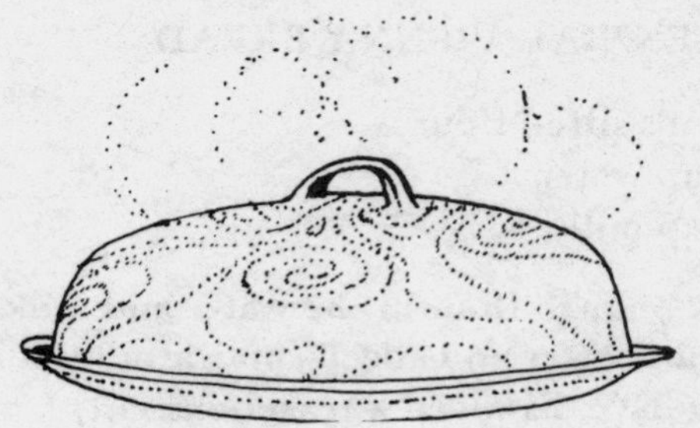

LORDS, LADIES AND BREAD

Anglo Saxon serfs had to be well fed if a manor was to prosper. Land owners whose land they worked were the men who "kept and gave out the bread," the lords. Their wives were "kneaders of dough" and "loaf givers" or ladies. The word loaf gave both these titles their first meaning.

This fact seemed reason enough to suggest that the art of bread making was "worth at least as much practice as a sonata (a piece of music)". The author of the statement was Dr. A. W. Chase who wrote the extraordinary old *Receipt Book and Household Physician or Practical Knowledge for the People – In Fact the Book for the Million.* The "third, last and complete memorial edition" of this book appeared in 1910.

This garrulous old fellow conducted an indefatigable search for recipes. In *Peterson's Ladies National Magazine,* he found a recipe for Vienna bread which he hastened to share. It was the very one, he said, that won acclaim at the Philadelphia Centennial.

CENTENNIAL VIENNA BREAD

8 cups sifted flour
1 cup water
1 cup milk

Mix enough flour in the water and milk to make a thin batter and add 1 cup warm milk in which you have dissolved 2 teaspoons salt, 1 tablespoon sugar and 3 level tablespoons yeast.

Set batter aside for 45 minutes. Then mix in remaining flour. Knead on a well floured board until dough is elastic and smooth. Half an hour of kneading was not too much in Grandmother's day but you can stop the minute the dough handles nicely, about 10 minutes. Dough should be neither sticky nor stiff. Place dough in a big bowl you can cover and let stand in a warm place for 2 – 2½ hours.

Butter your hands and divide raised dough into 3 pieces. Form them into loaves and set to rise again in well buttered pans. We save out one of these pieces for the Vienna Breakfast Bread below. Let rise until double in bulk and bake in a 375° oven for 30 minutes.

Yield: 3 loaves or 2 loaves and 1 Breakfast Bread

VIENNA BREAKFAST BREAD

This breakfast bread is definitely an experience to mix with your bare hands. When you finally get it into the mold – we use an ovenproof, clear glass 2-quart soufflé dish – you won't believe that the ropey, squooshy goo will turn into such a handsome, professional-looking loaf. When baked and cut, it looks like honeycomb. It makes delicious toast.

1 pound Vienna dough
2 tablespoons melted butter
½ cup powdered sugar
2 eggs

Beat all together in a bowl with your hands. Pour into plain mold to rise in a warm place for 45 minutes. Bake in 375° oven.

TRANSMITTED WITH LOVE AND AFFECTION

In his 98th and last year, Uncle Billie Crocker, custodian of sundry family treasures, gave into our hands Grandmother's cook book. He knew we would not only read it but use it and even share it, possibly, with you.

Here are a pair of lovelies that should evoke thoughts of crinoline, lavendar, and nosegays of violets and pink roses.

RICE BREAD

This bread is like nothing so much as a delicate rice custard pudding surprised in a popover. It is beautiful when it comes out of the oven and you feel terribly successful to have accomplished it! Serve hot, right from the oven. If there should be leftovers, reheat, tightly wrapped in aluminum foil, in a 350° oven for 25 minutes.

2 cups cooked rice
1 cup flour
4 eggs separated
2 tablespoons butter melted
2 cups milk
½ teaspoon salt

Mix rice, flour, lightly beaten yolks, butter, milk and salt. Beat egg whites to stiff froth and fold into batter. Bake in loaf pans or gem tins, 350° for 45 minutes in pans; less in gem tins.

Serves 4 hungry people; 6 otherwise!

ANISE TOAST

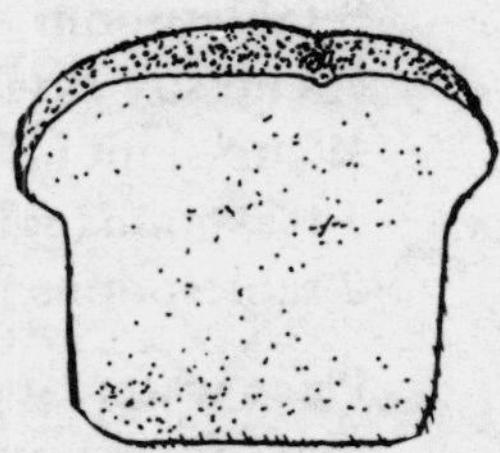

1 cup sugar
4 whole eggs, plus 2 yolks
2 tablespoons anise seeds
2 cups flour
Lemon flavoring to taste

In a double boiler over fire, beat eggs, yolks and sugar until light. Remove from heat and continue beating until cold.

Add flour, anise and flavoring. Spoon batter onto a buttered cookie sheet in long strips. Bake in a moderate oven. Cool and cut into slices and toast. Serve with coffee ice cream for dessert or with demitasse.

BREAD IS STILL MAKING HISTORY

In every age, emperors and average folk alike, have winked at ways to adulterate bread and the flour that went into making it. Because people early showed a preference for white bread, millers obliged by supplying whiter flour and inadvertently reduced its nutritive values.

Bread has often contained cosmetic properties designed to enhance its appeal as a package, not to create a supernutritional loaf. Bread flour has been chemically cured, bleached and standardized to improve the uniformity, volume and grain of loaves and rolls. Bread has been regimented to make all loaves look alike.

Sequestrants inactivate trace metals that affect flavor and color.

Surfactants keep liquids apart in baking process.

Buffers, acids and alkalies modify taste.

Bleaching and maturing agents remove yellow color from flour and improve its texture.

Preservatives prevent spoilage.

Some of these additives are now embattled.

MAKING IT GOOD AND LEGAL

In the 1940's, the move was on to restore the goodness of bread and bring back the thiamin, riboflavin, niacin and mineral iron absent in bleached white flour.

Laws in many states now require family flours to be so enriched as a result. And scientists have gone beyond the laws to find more ways to make bread a good food.

COLLEGE BRED BREAD

Most famous among them was the late Dr. Clive M. McCay who conducted experiments in bread nutrition. He and fellow researchers at Cornell University demonstrated that bread and butter could sustain life in health. The secret was the Cornell Triple Rich Formula.

A LITTLE SOMETHING YOU CAN ADD

Using the formula you can add three simple ingredients to each cup of flour to make a bread with superior nutritional quality:

1 tablespoon soy flour
1 tablespoon skim milk powder
1 teaspoon wheat germ

The scientists shared their findings with the baking industry only to have commercial bakers bring suit against them to prevent the formula from being used. The courts decided to allow the Cornell Mix Bread to be sold, provided it bore a label with all the ingredients – a condition not required for other breads.

Soy is richer in calcium and iron than regular wheat flour. Since it lacks gluten required to develop yeast doughs, it is not used alone. Many cooks use as much as 20 to 30% soy in bread recipes.

Here is the standard recipe for Cornell Bread. You can vary it by substituting stoneground whole wheat for some of the unbleached white flour. You can use brown sugar and add an egg and even brewer's yeast.

CORNELL BREAD

3 cups lukewarm water
2 tablespoons sugar or honey
2 tablespoons yeast
6 cups unbleached flour
3 tablespoons wheat germ
½ cup soy flour
¾ cup skim milk powder
4 teaspoons salt
2 tablespoons melted butter or margarine

Place water, sugar and yeast in large bowl. Let foam for 5 minutes. Sift flour, soy and milk powder together and stir in wheat germ. Stir salt into yeast mixture and add half the flour mix. Beat vigorously for several minutes. Stir in melted butter and remaining flour, adding an additional cup of flour if necessary.

Knead for 5 minutes. Put in covered, buttered bowl and let rise 45 minutes. Punch down. Turn

dough over and let rise another half hour. Turn out and divide into 3 pieces. Let rest 10 minutes. Shape into loaves and put into buttered pans. Cover and let rise until double in bulk. Bake in 350° oven 50 or 60 minutes. Cover with foil during last of baking if crusts appear to be browning too much.

Yield: 3 loaves

RESEARCH CONTINUES

Since Dr. McCay's day, research has continued in the effort to make bread better than ever. In 1972, a public patent for a new high protein bread formula showed how to blend up to 16% soy flour or any other high lysine concentrate with wheat flour. The process is said to boost protein content of white bread about 70% and to triple the concentration of lysine, an essential protein in human diets.

AN OMNIPRESENT WONDER BREAD

So lively is the interest in high protein health breads that recipes abound. We have found them everywhere — in newspapers, magazines and cook books. They are hand-written by friends who want to share them. We found this one among treasured recipes in a ladies aid society cook book. How fitting and full of faith that it should be called

MIRACLE BREAD

- 1 tablespoon yeast
- 1 cup warm water
- 3½ tablespoons powdered skim milk
- 2 tablespoons sugar
- 1 teaspoon salt
- 3 tablespoons soy flour
- ½ cup wheat germ
- 2 cups unbleached flour
- 2 tablespoons safflower oil

Dissolve yeast in warm water. Mix remaining ingredients and set to rise for one hour. Knead thoroughly and form loaf. Let rise again for 1 hour. Bake at 350° 30-35 minutes.

Yield: 1 loaf

This makes an excellent tasting, fine textured flattish loaf with a crisp crust. It makes very good toast.

Now it is your turn to make history with bread!

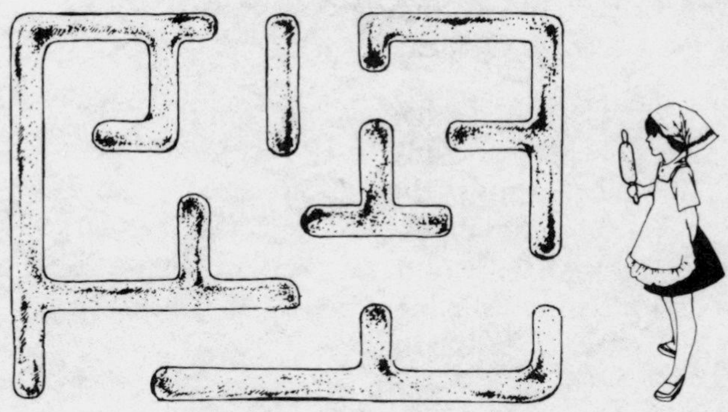

EXPERIMENTING

& BREAD STUFFS

On Being an Inventive Bread Baker

UNFORGETTABLE BREADS

How often have you finished a glorious meal with friends, then shared excited reminiscences about great things to eat, breads included?

Remember that raisin rye we had when we were kids? Wonder whatever happened to it. Toasted or untoasted, it was a treat and heaven spread with butter and peanut butter.

And that coal black rye we had at the big cocktail party? They cut it into tiny pieces just big enough to hold a piece of cheese. It tasted just like any other rye, but what a curiosity!

And that bread we found on the road in Gaspé country? Every few farms had a little stand built down by the highway. On it were maybe two loaves of bread wrapped in plastic. No one came down from the house to wait on us. We just took a loaf and left the money. It was delicious stuff and kept as good as new for a whole week.

And that cheese bread the home delivery bakery truck used to dispense in the neighborhoods eons ago? It, the bread, not the truck, was shaped like any ordinary loaf but it had this great cheese flavor. The company was called The People's Bakery.

And that marvelous whole wheat bread that looked like a lopsided chef's hat? We found it on Robson Street in Vancouver and they told us the dough had been compressed into the baking pan and weighted to hold it there. What a thick rich crust and what a fine texture! It, too, kept well like the bread from the Gaspé.

BEGUILING SHAPES, TOO

Well remembered breads have been shapely, too. There are the amusing turtles and alligators made from a sweet dough by a baker in Carmel, California.

And sour dough cow udder breads from a North Beach bakery in San Francisco. And French breads formed like Dungeness crabs and whole salmons with lifelike scales. And Ukrainian breads with charming doves on top.

CAN YOU MAKE THEM?

Inevitably, the adventurous ask, "Do you think we can make them ourselves?"

Of course, you can!

Bakers aren't likely to share the basis for their livelihood with you. But there is a way. Simply buy breads that appeal to you and learn about them by eating them.

Some breads list enough ingredients on their wrappers to give you a good start on devising your own recipe and adding a few frills in the process. And if they don't have wrappers, ask questions.

On our travels we have asked students, young marrieds and even the man on the street, "Where can we buy the most interesting bread in your city?" If several give the same answer, we investigate.

In Victoria, a young travel agent recommended Squirrelly Bread. In many other cities, the source of imaginative breads has been health food stores.

A BREAD BAZAAR

Over the years, one of the most fascinating bread emporiums we have ever patronized has been the Seattle Tastie Home Bakery.

Don't let the trite name deflect you! This bakery needs its parking lot. It is always buzzing with customers. Its staples are like few others.

The first thing you see is a big bread carte, carrying at last count 21 breads. Very obligingly, the bakery will make any bread you want, provided you order a minimum of six loaves.

THE BREAD CARTE

Half the breads listed are fairly common — corn bread, stick French bread, egg sesame bread and bread that is salt free. The interesting aspect of the bread carte is its hint of possibilities for experimentation. Consider these.

Farm Bread made with white flour, corn meal, butter and honey.

Honey Vita, a square loaf made with pure honey, vegetable juices, stoneground wheat, wheat germ.

A RECIPE FOR GARGANTUA

Nature Plus Here you have to stop because the list of ingredients boggles the mind. You suddenly have the feeling that if you are brave enough to order a loaf or intrepid enough to bake one, you will not be able to lift it. But read on, for you can lift it!

Nature Plus contains enriched wheat flour, millet, stoneground wheat, yeast, lecithin, rolled oats, sunflower, rye, corn meal, soy, carob meal, bran, sugar, vegetable shortening, milk powder, sea salt, barley, beans, lentils, fennel and spelt.

The carte continues:

Grandma's Molasses, coarse ground wheat

Poppin Wheat with ground raisins that pop when toasted

100% Raisin has a pound of raisins for every pound of dough.

Limpa Rye with cardamon and raisins

English Muffin Bread, excellent for toast

A MOUNTAIN OF INGREDIENTS OR A MEAL IN A SLICE!

Ecology Bread. This may be heavy with ingredients, but it is a surprisingly fine textured and mild lightweight. In a single bread you find unbleached Montana wheat, non-fat milk, wheat bran, cracked wheat, yellow corn meal, whole wheat, gluten flour, lecithin, salt, soy flour, milk, sugar, pure vegetable shortening, rye, barley, flax, natural brown raw sugar, potato flour, molasses and rolled oats!

UNLIMITED IMAGINATION

Potential experiments do not stop with trying such free-wheeling breads as Ecology Bread and Nature Plus.

Victoria's Squirrelly Bread packs into its loaves sunflower seeds, sprouted 100% whole wheat kernels, malt, dulse (a coarse sea weed), kelp and unsulphured molasses.

Elsewhere we found a Homestead Loaf that eschewed preservatives and was made from organic sprouted grains of wheat, oats, rye, corn, millet, soybean, barley and well water among other things. Unfortunately the Homestead mix did not come off as a bread so much as a brick packed with grains that were dry and harsh and tough to chew. The stuff will not slice well. It crumbles in the hand.

This is not to say that good bread can't come from such a combination of ingredients. We once enjoyed a hearty bread — which did hold together when cut — and which was made from grain ground from cattle feed. When the ground grain would not come together, the young baker added a goose egg and a duck egg. Presto! A good loaf, a memorable bread.

A CAUTION

We find it a good idea to start with a basic recipe for white or whole wheat or rye bread and use it as a foundation for experiments. And go easily when you find a recipe you like that seems to invite experiments with additional or even different flours, textural bread stuffs and nutritional additives.

Use a spoonful of this or ¼ cup of that. Use leftover mashed potatoes and squash in the refrigerator to add their texture and color to bread. Add a couple of spoonfuls of brewer's yeast to the measuring cup before adding flour called for in your recipe. Try to find a bread recipe something like the bread you want to reproduce. You may not reproduce exactly what a baker baked but you will come close. Sometimes you will even surpass him.

Breads We Had Fun Experimenting With

PUMPERNICKEL WITH RAISINS

The inspiration for this bread as well as another one we tried later was a pumpernickel bread we had in Fresno, chocked full of raisins. We combed Fresno all one morning trying to buy some for the freezer but all the natives had bought up the supply everywhere we went! We went home without it and resolved to make our own. This is how we did it.

2 tablespoons yeast
1/4 cup dark molasses
1/4 cup lukewarm water
3 tablespoons melted butter
1 cup scalded buttermilk
1/4 teaspoon soda
1 teaspoon salt
1/2 cup mashed potatoes
1 cup dark rye flour
1 3/4 cups whole wheat flour
1 cup buckwheat flour
1/4 cup soy flour
2 cups seedless raisins

Dissolve yeast in warm water with molasses. Combine butter, scalded buttermilk, soda, salt

and mashed potatoes. When mix is lukewarm, add to yeast mix. Stir in rye and half the whole wheat. Mix thoroughly. Add buckwheat and soy and turn out onto board and knead with remaining whole wheat for 8 – 10 minutes. Knead in raisins last and set to rise in covered bowl in warm place until double in bulk – about 1 hour. Punch down and let rise another 30 minutes. Form into round loaves and place on well buttered sheet dusted with corn meal. Let rise again for about 45 minutes. Bake in moderate 350° oven for 1 hour.

Yield: 2 medium loaves

Notes. This bread has a homely, satisfying taste and is perfectly delicious spread with cream cheese. It has a good crust, is finely textured and sweet with all those raisins.

Another way to make pumpernickel, we discovered, is to use leftover buckwheat pancake batter. We used the same recipe above, cut back on yeast, molasses and butter and used a cupful of batter instead of 1 cup of buckwheat flour. The resulting bread was excellent and had a more tender crust.

Pumpernickel recipes often call for corn meal. Some use whole bran cereal and even melted, unsweetened chocolate (2 squares). Chocolate would certainly give pumpernickel the Fresno look, though we didn't detect chocolate in the taste.

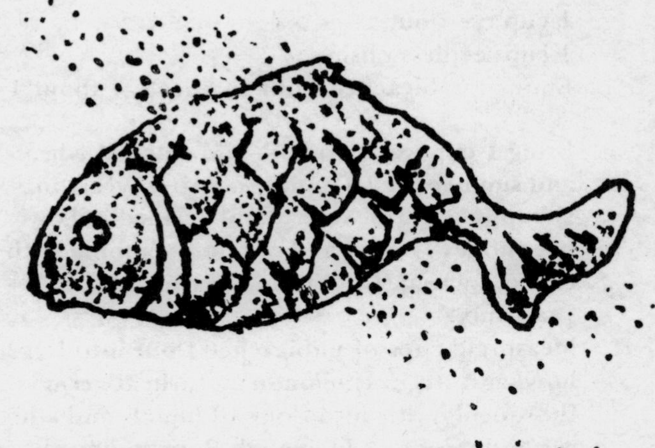

HONEY RAISIN RYE

What about that raisin bread we loved when we were small – the rye bread with its hint of spice? How to make that? This is the way we finally reconstructed it.

1 cup water
1/4 cup cracked wheat
1 tablespoon yeast
1/4 cup lukewarm water
1/2 cup scalded milk
1/3 cup honey
2 tablespoons butter
1/2 teaspoon salt
2 cups unbleached flour
1/2 teaspoon cinnamon
2 teaspoons wheat germ

1 cup rye flour
1 cup seedless raisins
Enough unbleached flour to knead – about 1 cup

Bring 1 cup water to boil, add cracked wheat and simmer for 10 minutes. Soften yeast in ¼ cup lukewarm water. Pour scalded milk over honey, butter and salt and combine with cracked wheat. Cool to lukewarm and add yeast mix.
Measure 2 cups of unbleached flour into large bowl and stir in cinnamon and wheat germ thoroughly. Stir into flour all liquids and add rye and raisins. Add enough flour to knead dough. Knead until smooth and elastic. Set to rise in covered bowl in warm place for 1 hour or until double in bulk. Punch down vigorously. Form a round loaf and let rise in round buttered layer cake pan until double in bulk. Bake at 350° for 40 minutes.

Yield: 1 two-pound loaf

Note. This recipe produces a moist, very fragrant loaf, redolent of honey when it comes from the oven. The cracked wheat assures a nutlike texture.

SAVING GRACES

Assured for a long time of the near indestructibility of bread doughs, we have forged ahead and tried many things. This includes introducing leftovers. One of the most pleasant of these was banana squash.

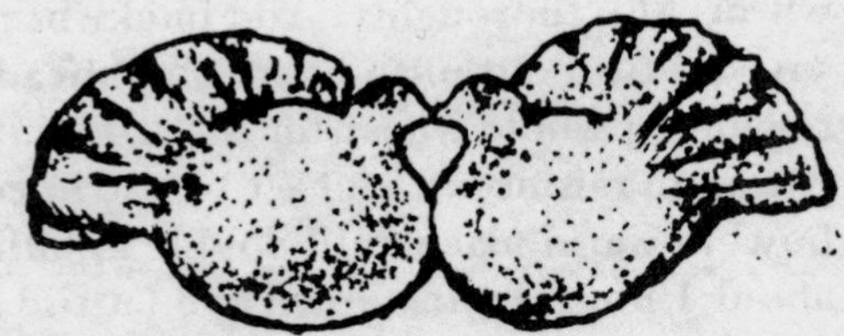

SQUASH BREAD

Mix 1 cup cooked, puréed squash with 1½ cups scalded milk. Cool to lukewarm. Add 1 tablespoon yeast, 2 tablespoons sugar, 1 tablespoon butter and ¼ cup water. Beat well. Add 1 teaspoon salt in 5 cups of unbleached flour and enough additional flour to knead. Knead vigorously for 10 minutes.

Set dough to rise in warm place in covered bowl until double in bulk – about 1½ hours. Punch down and divide into 2 pieces to form loaves. Place in buttered bread pans and allow to rise until double in bulk. Bake in a moderate oven 30 – 40 minutes.

Yield: 2 large loaves

Notes. This makes a delicious, slightly sweet bread. You cannot identify the squash at all. It disappears, leaving its sunny yellow color and giving the loaf an amiable delicacy. When we sent a friend off with a loaf, she wrote back, "I still have half a loaf of the squash bread. I cut it in extravagantly thick slices, lavish it with butter and cheese and eat it with great relish."

Also useful in achieving interesting tastes and color are mashed turnips; potatoes, both Irish and sweet; pumpkin; and puréed chestnuts, zucchini, beans, artichoke hearts, asparagus and carrots.

DON'T DESERT THE SLOW DOUGH!

BREAD WITH GROUND WHEAT SPROUTS OR COOKED CEREALS

This bread brought us to the conclusion that bread, like many growing things will come into being and flourish even when the maker is awkward and amateurish and the bread dough is strange!

When the dough was laggard in rising, we said to each other, "Well, if this takes much longer (two hours had already elapsed), we'll just have to start over." And we went off and forgot it in its "warm, draft-free" place to continue rising. When we next remembered the dough, six hours had passed! But the dough had doubled in size finally and at long last we got it into the oven to bake. The result was a round loaf, 7 inches in diameter and 3 inches high. It had a nice sweet/sour flavor, a fine chewy texture unlike any bread we had made before.

¾ cup warmed ground sprouted wheat
¼ cup brown sugar
½ teaspoon salt
1 tablespoon melted butter
1 tablespoon yeast dissolved in
¼ cup lukewarm water
1¾ cups unbleached flour

Combine sprouted wheat, sugar, salt and butter. Add dissolved yeast and flour. Knead well. Place in a covered bowl and let rise until double in bulk. Be patient! Punch down and shape into round loaf and let rise in a buttered ovenproof casserole. Bake at 350° for 25-30 minutes.

Notes. You can buy wheat seeds for sprouting in health food stores as well as special wide mouth jars with screens and instructions on how to sprout. Some view sprouts as highly nutritious sources of quick energy with excellent vitamin content, especially of C and B complex. In any case, the recipe above makes a fine loaf that cuts well.

The same recipe lends itself to cooked cereals – leftover oatmeal, cream of wheat, 7-grain cereal and even plain rice. Here is an opportunity to innovate. Just substitute 1 cup of warm cooked cereal for the wheat sprouts and use 2¼ cups of unbleached flour. The dough will be a bit deceiving. You'll wonder how it can absorb 2¼ cups flour, but it can! The finished bread is light and delicious.

BARLEY BREAD WITH CHEESE

Barley bread recalls Aesop's immortal fable of the country and the city mouse. After a shattering visit to the city, the country mouse advised his luxury-loving friend that he preferred barley bread in peace and security in his humble home to tasting the daintiest food in a splendid mansion.

Appropriately enough the San Diego Children's Zoo connects bread and mice, too. It has one of the most enchanting bread exhibits in the world – a Mouse House made of an outsized loaf of bread. In it dwells a lively colony of tunneling mice.

We added cheese to our barley bread recipe. With the eggs it produces a creamy yellow bread which, though it is tender, has an interesting, chewy texture.

2 tablespoons yeast
½ cup lukewarm water
1¼ cups scalded milk
2 tablespoons sugar
½ teaspoon salt
½ cup safflower oil
2½ cups unbleached flour
2 beaten eggs
½ cup cheddar cheese, grated
1½ cups barley flour
Flour to make a stiff dough

Let yeast foam in lukewarm water. In a large bowl combine sugar, salt and shortening with scalded milk. Beat in unbleached flour and beaten eggs. Stir in softened yeast, grated cheese and barley flour.

Add enough unbleached flour to make stiff dough and knead until smooth and elastic, about 10 minutes. Place in buttered bowl to rise in warm place until double in bulk. Punch down and let rest 10 minutes. Divide dough in half and form 2 round loaves and place in buttered 9-inch cake pans to rise again until double in bulk. Bake at 350° for 35-40 minutes.

Yield: 2 loaves

Note. We saved out a spoonful of dough to make a big-eared, long-tailed mouse for the last rising. Of course we used mouse-catching anise seeds for eyes. When mouse and round loaf had cooled, we attached the mouse to the top of the loaf with a toothpick.

TO GIVE BREAD A BETTER RELISH

Something very ancient and elemental in herbs satisfies the recurrent yearning we all have to stay hunger with a food that is just plain good. Yet few cooks, even those with knowledge of fresh and dried herbs, have come forward with bread recipes requiring herbs and herb seeds. Obviously this area is ready for ideas unlimited.

At least seventeen herbs are worth considering when you make your next bread:

Spicy anise that makes a confection of bread; sweet scented basil; nippy carraway; warming celery seeds; flattering fennel; that mild onion, the antique chive; fragrant coriander; cumin; dill seeds with their anti-witch magic; marjoram, joy of the mountains; quickening mustard seed; healthy parsley; sympathetic sage; soothing savory; aromatic little dragon of a tarragon; and fine flavored thyme. To say nothing of rosemary and sesame.

FLATTERING FENNEL BREAD

The origin of this bread is Hungarian. Its taste is most palatable.

4 – 5 cups unsifted flour
2 teaspoons sugar
1 teaspoon salt
2½ teaspoons fennel seeds
2 tablespoons yeast
2 tablespoons softened butter
1¾ cups very hot tap water

Corn meal
1 egg yolk
2 teaspoons cream or milk

Thoroughly mix 1½ cups flour, sugar, salt, 1 teaspoon fennel and undissolved yeast in large bowl. Add butter. Slowly add tap water to dry ingredients and beat vigorously for 2 minutes. Add another ½ cup flour or enough to make thick batter and continue beating vigorously. Stir in enough flour to make soft dough and turn out onto lightly floured board. Knead until smooth, about 8-10 minutes. Place in buttered bowl, turning to butter top. Cover and let rise in warm place until double in bulk, about 30 minutes.

Punch down and divide in half. Shape 2 round balls and place at opposite ends of buttered

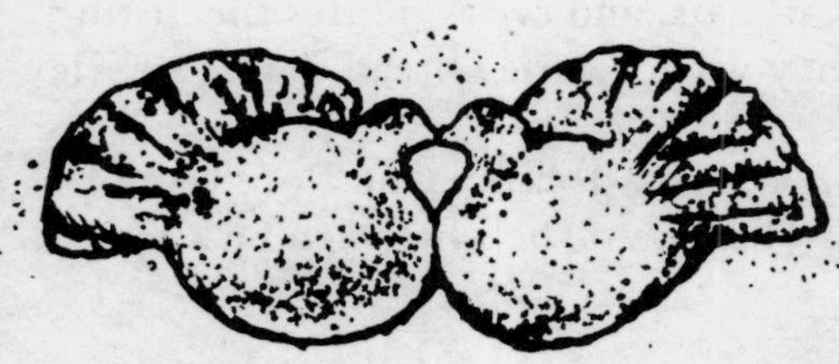

baking sheet sprinkled with corn meal. Let rise until doubled.

Beat egg yolk and cream and brush on loaves. Sprinkle remaining 1½ teaspoons fennel on loaves and bake in 400° oven until done, about 30 minutes.

Notes. Easy Does It! Herbs are the easiest of all taste altering stuffs to add to bread mixes. You can start by introducing your favorite herb to the flour first by the half teaspoon, then more, depending on how the finished bread strikes you. Some exceptions are these: you can use somewhat more basil, chervil and marjoram. With herb seeds you can allow even more, especially if you put them in the dough and sprinkle them on top the loaf in baking. These amounts are for recipes producing two loaves of bread.

YOU CAN MAKE A BLEND OF DRIED HERBS

Blend well equal amounts of marjoram, rosemary, savory, oregano, thyme and parsley. Add small amounts of basil, sage and chervil. Mix well and hold in airtight container. Use 1-3 tablespoons for a 2-loaf recipe.

A combination we especially like is for a 1-loaf Irish soda bread: ¼ teaspoon each of marjoram and oregano, ½ teaspoon basil and a pinch of thyme.

Another recipe that promises good, hearty eating requires 2 tablespoons dried parsley or chives, 1/8 teaspoon crumbled rosemary and ½ teaspoon sage.

And why not try to make a bread sometime with leftover mashed carrots and flavor it with lemon thyme?

STANDARDS FOR CREATIVITY AND EATABILITY

When you are creating a new bread, your goals are very personal. How you mix flours and bread stuffs depends on your purpose. You may be aiming for a distinctive flavor and appearance; improved nutritive and energy values; reduced calorie count. You may want to make a bread that is highly digestible, that avoids an allergy problem, or that just makes efficient use of a few leftovers.

JOHNNY-ONE-NOTE vs FULL CONCERT

Some purists believe in following that principle of great art that directs that one flour or breadstuff predominate. For them, the mixture of several flours – wheat, oats, and rye – dilutes the distinctive taste. They want a barley bread that is a barley bread.

Others abhor such a Johnny-One-Note way of doing things. They want their bread to be a sym-

phony of tastes at full concert level. They want, as one experimenter explained it, "to wipe out my tastebuds!"

"I want the fun of tasting a number of flavors, of searching out and identifying each and getting a whole new experience from a multi-taste, multi-textured bread. That kind of bread is greater than the sum of its parts. That's serendipity!

"For instance, I like cinnamon. But I always add orange peel and apple. And I find that 1 to 1½ cups of corn meal adds a great texture to any loaf."

New Entity Bread Game

Components that go into making bread are organized below under ten headings. Accompanying each is a listing of possible alternatives.

The object of the game is to discover among these lists possible elements you can use to create a once only, tradition-defying loaf every time you bake.

Note this ploy: To win, you need only introduce or vary one element in a recipe to achieve something new.

1 RAISING DOUGH

Stratagem: Raise the dough differently.

By Yeast: Dry or Compressed	Salt Rising	Starters:	Baking Powder	Baking Soda	Malt Mash	Homemade Yeast
		Sourdough Wheat Rye Potato				

2 FLOURS & OTHER CEREAL BREAD STUFFS

*Stratagem: Devise a new flour arrangement.**

Cereals, Cooked:	Dry Cereals, Moistened:	Ground Sprouted Seeds:	
Farina Oatmeal Multi-grain, etc.	All bran Grapenuts Shredded Wheat, etc.	Wheat Alfalfa Soy beans	Barley Millet Rye, etc.

3 LIQUIDS

Stratagem: Substitute other liquids for water and milk.

Water:	Milk:	Eggs:	Fruit Juices:
Tap, well, and rain water	Sour, fresh, canned, buttermilk, sour cream, yogurt	Chicken, duck, goose, turkey, ostrich	Apple, apricot, cherry, grape, orange and pineapple

**See FLOUR ARRANGEMENT CHART, pgs. 26~29.*

Liquids continued.

Soups:	Beverages:	Alcohol:	Vegetable Juices:	Other:
Meats	Coffee	Wines	Carrot	Vinegars
Poultry	Tea	Liqueurs (diluted)	Soy Milk	Pickle juice
Potato	Soda Water	Beer	Tomato	
	Ginger beer	Brandy	Liquids left over from cooking and steaming vegetables	
		Rum		

4 FATS

Stratagem: Innovate with butter, margarine, low cholesterol cooking and salad oils, bacon drippings, rendered chicken fat.

5 COLORS

Stratagem: Use colorful stuff.

Egg yolks
Mashed pumpkins and squash
Highly colored juices and beverages
Artificial food coloring, etc.

6 MISCELLANEOUS STUFF

Stratagem: Alter taste and texture.

Fruits and Vegetables:

Apple
Apricot
Avocado
Currant
Banana
Berries
Cherry
Crabapple
Cranberry
Date
Fig
Grape
Mango

Cooked, mashed or pureed:
- Artichoke Hearts
- Beans
- Beets
- Cabbages
- Carrots
- Garbanzos
- Mushrooms
- Onions
- Peas
- Potatoes

Nuts and Seeds:

Almonds
Almond Paste
Aniseed
Brazil Nuts
Caraway
Cashews
Chestnuts
Coconut
Flax Seed
Hazelnuts
Hickory Nuts
Peanuts & Peanut Butter

Cheeses:

Blue
Cottage
Cheddar
Cream
Parmesan
Swiss, etc.

Nutritional Additives:

Brewer's Yeast
Milk Solids
Instant Whey
Dried Buttermilk
Gelatins, Plain & Flavored
Dry Soup Mixes
Other

Fruits and Vegetables:

Olive
Papaya
Peaches
Pear
Pineapple
Plum
Prune
Quince
Raisin
Pumpkin
Squash
Turnips
Yams
Other

Nuts and Seeds:

Pecans
Pine Nuts
Walnuts

Other Seeds:
Dill
Fennel
Poppyseed
Sesame

Cooked Meats, Fish:

Bacon
Fish
Fowl
Ham
Shrimp
Other

7 SEASONINGS, FLAVORINGS & SWEETENERS

Stratagem: Modify flavors and aroma.

Herbs, Spices, Etc:

Basil
Cardamon
Carob Powder
Cloves
Cocoa
Coffee
Extracts:
- Almond
- Anise
- Lemon

Mint
Nutmeg
Onion & Garlic
Parsley
Rinds:
- Grapefruit
- Lemon
- Orange

Sea Salt & Weed
Tarragon
Thyme
Vanilla

Sweeteners:

Cane Syrup
Coconut Honey
Honey
Jams
Jellies
Malt Extract
Malted Milk Powder
Maple Syrup
Marmalade
Molasses
Sorghum
Various Sugars

Dried Fruits; Candies:

Chocolate Chips
Licorice
Marshmallow
Ginger
Glace Fruits —
- Citron
- Cherry
- Lemon
- Orange

Gumdrops
Watermelon Rind
Mincemeat

8 FORM DURING FINAL RISING

Stratagem: Be a bread sculptor.

Pans That Shape

Bundt
Spring forms
Casseroles
Round cake pans
1 lb. & 2 lb.
coffee cans
#1 flat cans
Cookie cutters
Rabbits
Birds
Deer, etc.

Fluted pans
Brioche pans

Traditional Shapes

Round
Square
Rectangular
Triangular
Star
Heart
Cylinder
Loaf

In Round Pans:

Wreaths and flat breads with hole in center.

On Flat Sheets:

Knots.
Roll dough out and pull out into rope. Tie knots and figure 8's

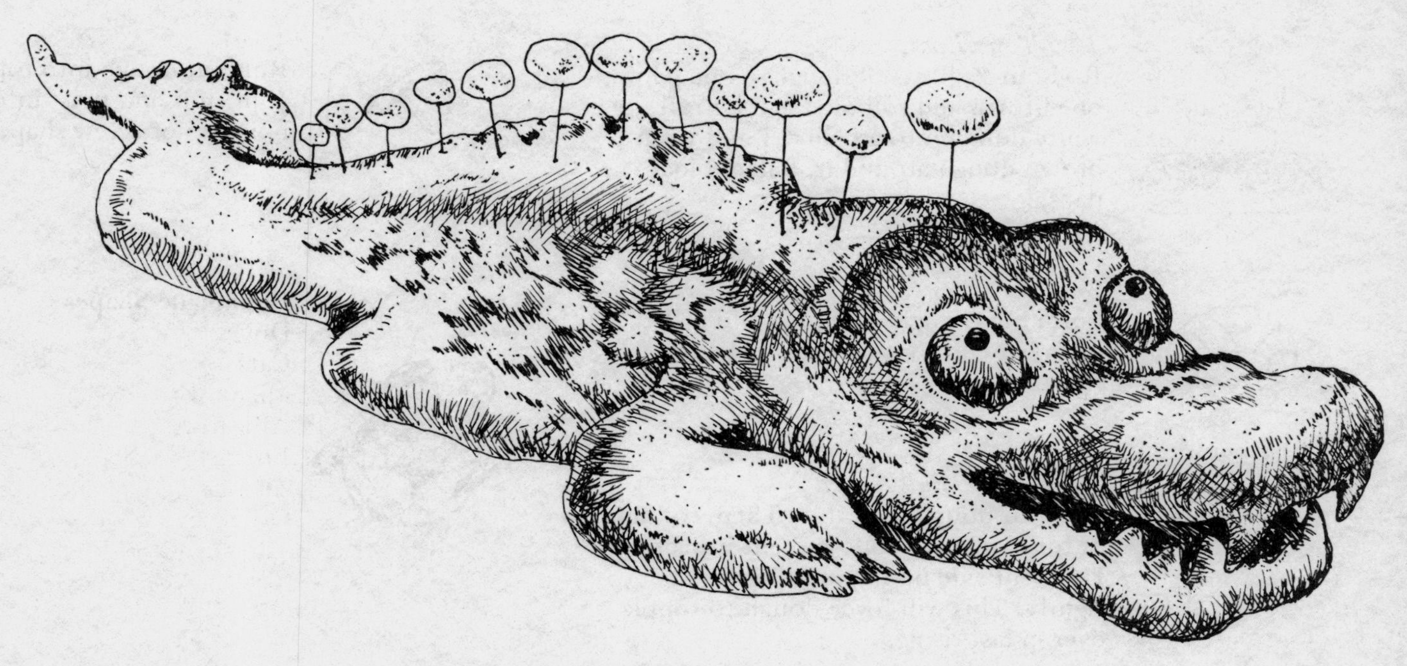

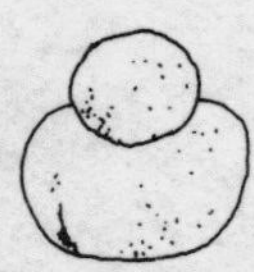

Stacks
Cottage Loaf.
Two layer
Large round ball of dough on bottom topped by smaller ball of dough.

Pyramid.
Same as Cottage Loaf with 3 or more balls of dough ascending from large to small.

Assemblies
Tear-Apart Loaves.
Crowd balls of dough into rectangular pan.

Two-Tone Loaf.
Roll out 2 sheets of dough – one white, one brown and roll or stack. Or roll white dough into a cylinder and wrap brown dough around it. Bake in loaf pans.

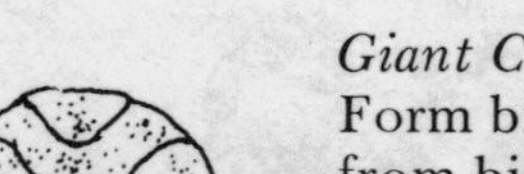

Giant Croissant.
Form big triangle of dough and roll from big end to small end. Bake on sheet.

Toppleover, Pull-Apart.
Roll out dough very thin. Then, roll up as for cinnamon rolls and cut in sections. Place cut side up in pan, filling pan tightly. This will force dough to topple over in last rising.

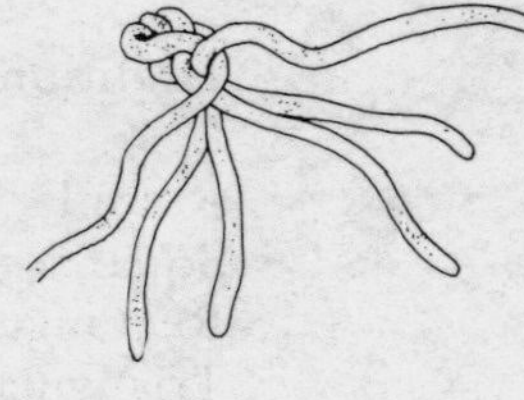

Braids.
Form long dough ropes (2–6 of them) and plait. Use 2 kinds of dough, white and brown, just to be different. You can also use large braids on bottom and smaller ones on top.

Coils.
Use one long rope of dough. Form into a spiral that thins toward top.

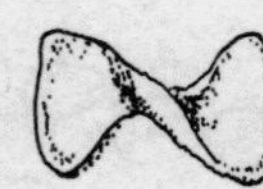

Twists.
Roll out dough into ropes. Join ends and twist into bow ties or screw shapes.

Handmade Shapes
Doves
Cats
Mice
Alligators
Fish
Turtles
Other

9 DECORATIONS
Stratagem: Be incisive. Use knives and scissors.

Crisscross ✕

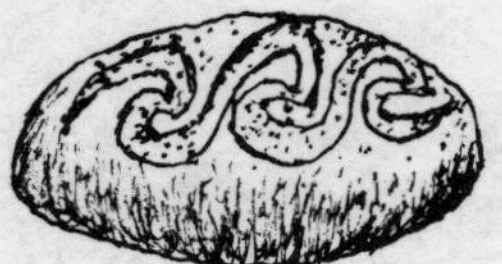
Easter Egg Symbols

Notches

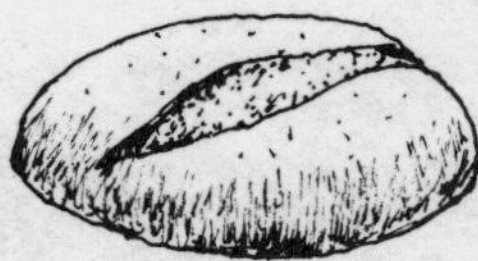
Slash

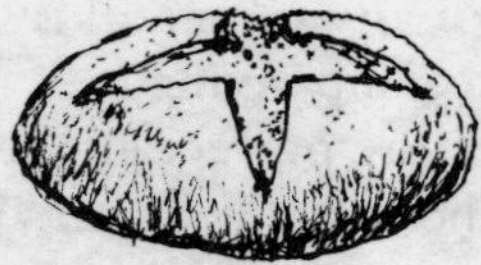
Cross +

Herringbone

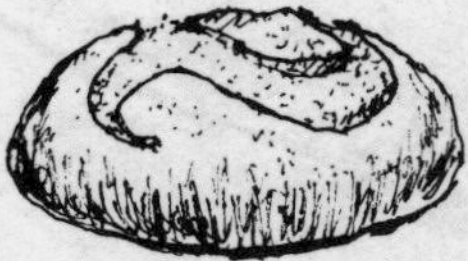
Scroll

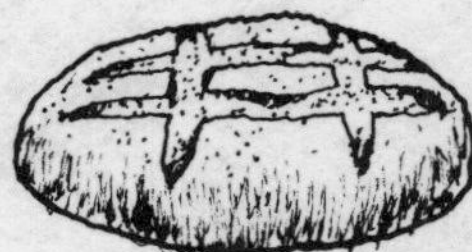
Ticktacktoe #

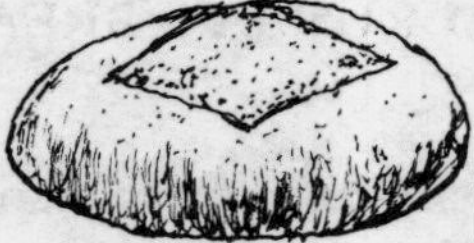
Diamond ◆

Leaf Cut

Shamrock

10 GLAZES & FINISHING TOUCHES
Stratagem: Dress it up!

Dust with flour

Use egg wash and sprinkle with:
Chopped nuts
Sesame seeds
Poppy seeds
Meal flakes
Herbs
Dried onions

Brush on Flavorings and Sweetenings:

Sugar and milk
Water & molasses
Fruit juices
Wine & sugar
Yeast paste of:
Yeast, sugar, water, cornstarch or rice flour and oil (for Dutch Crunch effect)

Brush on fat

Butter
Salad oil
Lard
Margarine

Various

Milk wash
Water spray
Water & Postum
Water & Cornstarch

BREADS FOR ALL SEASONS

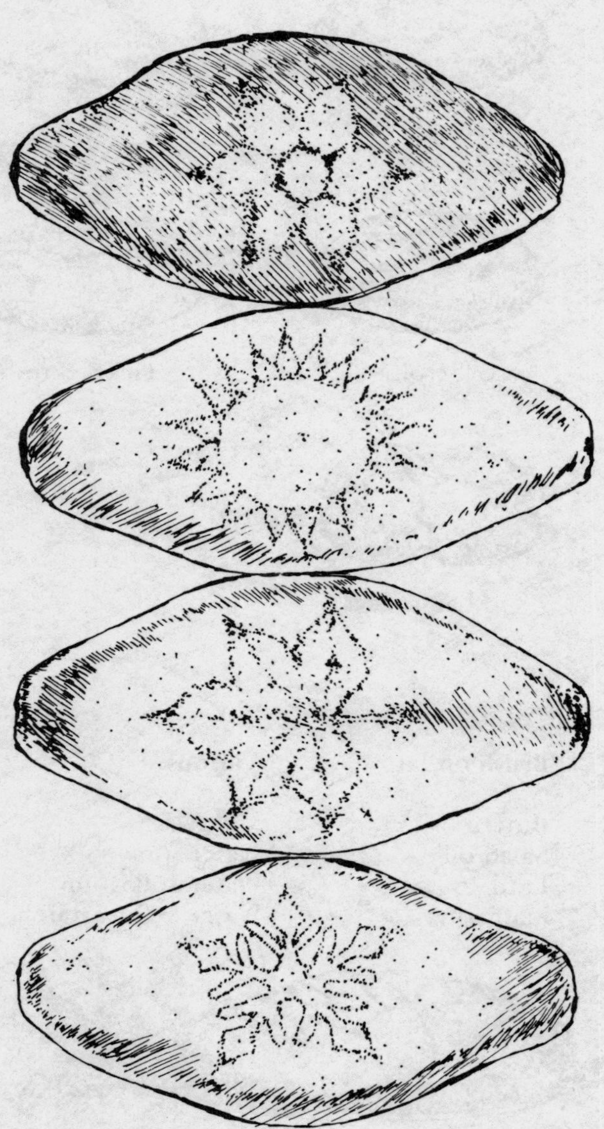

BREAD AS A GIFT

In our very marrow are Lowell's "The gift without the giver is bare" and Mother's precept that the most important part of any gift at all is the personal message or effort accompanying it.

Believing so, what more perfect gift can anyone bear to a friend than homemade bread? What better compliment than to receive a handmade loaf as a gift?

TRADITIONS FROM RUSSIA'S BREAD BASKET

Breads of all kinds are intimately associated with holidays, festivals and landmark events marking human history.

Some of the most beautiful bread traditions anywhere developed early in the Ukraine. The abundance of excellent wheat was matched with an abundance of ingenious bakers. Their culinary skills have been legendary.

In the middle of the 19th Century, Balzac who married Evelina, Countess Hanska, and lived with her for several years near Kiev took note of them in a letter to a friend.

"Perhaps one day," he wrote, "I will be able to repay you this friendly service when you come to Ukraine, this terrestrial paradise, where I marked 77 ways of preparing bread, which fact itself suggests the idea that the people are able to manipulate even the simplest things."

WELCOMING GESTURE

In the Ukraine it is the custom never to go visiting empty handed. A common gift is a loaf of bread.

When the Virsky Ukrainian State Dance Ensemble visited United States and Canada, dancers offered bread and salt in a gesture of welcome and friendship. Loaves of bread lying on long embroidered towels were brought forward by two young women who, bowing to left and right, said, "We are from Ukraine."

In general the custom today is observed by organizations greeting church dignitaries and people of distinction.

FOR LANDMARK CELEBRATIONS

Bread has been an important symbol in landmark celebrations at every stage of life. Each bread has its name, distinctive shape, special dough decorations and symbolism. A braided bread both blesses a newlywed pair and symbolizes eternity for the departed.

In times past, a bread and salt ritual ushered a newlywed couple to their new home. This Kalach, this braided ring-shaped bread, derives its name from the Ukrainian word for circle — an ancient symbol of good luck, prosperity, bountiful life and general welfare as well as eternity.

These breads that are more than bread played a role in one's life even before he arrived in this world. The expectant father sought out an older woman to be midwife and presented her with a loaf. In accepting it, she agreed to serve, as she had to. When the time came, she arrived with a loaf of bread and bowed thirty times before icons in the home. Following the birth, she buried the placenta beneath the earthen floor along with a piece of the bread and a small coin. Over all she strewed wheat.

The choice of godparents was another occasion for bread. The father or a stand-in came bearing a loaf. Acceptance of the proffered loaf and a reciprocal gift of bread settled the matter. The godparents also brought bread to the christening.

BETROTHALS

A very special bread marked engagements. Matchmakers approached a girl's parents with a bottle of whiskey; a cane symbolic of the diplomatic nature of the errand; and bread.

With initial courtesies over, the matchmaker kissed the bread and handed it to the father of the family. If he accepted the proposal, he kissed the bread, placed it on the table and served it to the matchmaker. If he refused it, the bread was returned to the matchmaker.

At the betrothal, the couple bowed low to the parents who blessed them with a loaf of bread — sometimes with two loaves united.

THE MARRIAGE BREAD

The bride-to-be with her bridesmaids personally delivered invitations to the wedding. She bore a bread baked in the shape of a pine cone and often decorated with ribbons and a spray of berries from the guelder rose. When they returned home, they trooped around the family table. On it was an embroidered cloth and a loaf of bread at each corner. The bride-to-be paused before each, bowed and kissed the loaves.

For the wedding there was another very special bread, Korovai. Its ceremonial use harks back to ancient times when people discarded ritual sacrifice of animals for offerings of seeds, scented grasses and bread.

Originally a product full of the magic of the number seven, Korovai promoted happiness and good fortune. On it were symbols of the sun and moon and representations of doves and animals.

Seven different fields produced grain for the flour. Seven different sacks conveyed it. Seven times three score eggs were kneaded into the dough. Seven white hens laid the eggs. Seven churns made the butter for the loaf from the milk of seven young cows. Seven wells provided water for the dough. Seven young women, all happily married, prepared the bread.

To the accompaniment of music, the matchmaker and bridesmaids bore the finished bread into the fields to gather periwinkle. On their return, they thrust a knife into the center of the loaf, tied a string to it and braided periwinkle stems to it. This wreath decorated the bread. With the decorated bread, the bride's parents blessed her before the ceremony.

Bread symbolism did not stop there. The bride's hair was braided with bread. Before leaving for the church, she was blessed with bread. As she bid farewell, her family received her, all seated in a row on a bench, their laps covered with a long embroidered shawl. On each lap was a small loaf of bread. The bride bowed to each kinsman, kissed him and the breads.

Wedding rites featured bread. Elders held small loaves over the head of the couple, or the godmother of the bride held a loaf on the bride's shoulder during the ceremony.

Korovai is still very much a part of wedding feasts. You will find a recipe below that will spare you the intricacies of the "rule of seven."

EVERYMAN'S FESTIVE BREADS

The rush of time, the practical non-existence of national borders and the freedom of communication have put us all in possession of breads from everywhere. Breads traditionally enjoyed on special occasions for festivals and holidays make their appearance the year round and even wait for us on supermarket shelves.

Frankly, we felt cheated when Panettone, that lovely Italian stuff, no longer waited for Christmas. The little plump loaves that made welcome gifts in late December became too common to give away — unless we took the initiative and made it ourselves!

And that is what we propose to do before all these beautiful breads suffer a low destiny and become common fare, before they become homogenized and lose their identity.

A PAIR OF UKRAINIAN BREADS

KOROVAI, THE WEDDING BREAD WITH BIRDS AND BRAIDS ON TOP

1 teaspoon sugar	2½ cups warm water
½ teaspoon ginger	4 beaten eggs
½ cup warm water	1 tablespoon salt
2 tablespoons yeast	3 tablespoons sugar
	3 tablespoons oil
	8½ cups flour or more

Dissolve sugar, ginger and yeast in warm water. Add to beaten eggs, salt, sugar, 2½ cups water, and oil. Add flour. Knead until smooth. Dough should be a little stiffer than for the usual bread. Place in a buttered bowl, cover and let rise until double in bulk.

Put aside a good handful of dough and refrigerate until you are ready to make birds.

Use a tube pan for the bread, buttering it well. Roll out enough dough to fill bottom quarter of the pan. Shape another portion into three rolls about 36 inches long and ¾ inch thick. Braid these rolls, join the ends and place them on top of the dough in the pan.

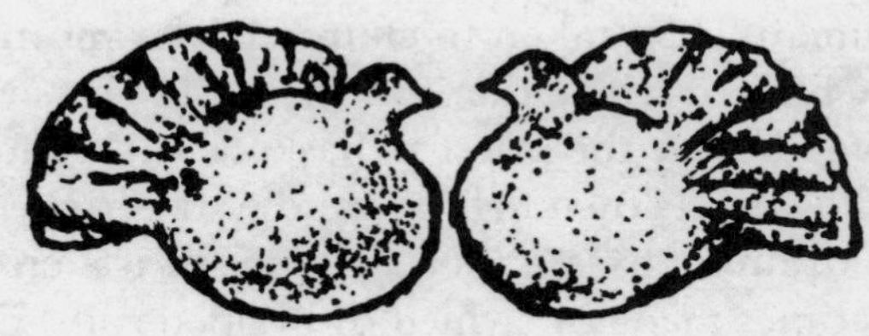

Shape another portion of dough into two shorter rolls and twine them. Join the ends and place them around the inside of the tube pan. Put in a warm place to rise until double in bulk and glaze with beaten egg yolk and milk. Bake at 325° for 20 minutes and increase heat to 350° and bake another hour or until golden.

Now, get the dough you have been holding in the refrigerator and shape into rolls ½ inch thick. Cut into strips about 4½ inches long. Tie knot and shape a head at one end and flatten the other end for a tail, making 4 cuts with a knife to fan out a tail.

Make small birds for the rim and larger ones for center. Bake on buttered sheet at 350° for 15-20 minutes. Use poppy seeds or other dark whole spice for eyes. Place birds on finished bread, using toothpicks to secure them.

Yield: 1 large loaf

PASKA

Paska is an Easter bread with intricate dough ornaments. It is taken to church Easter morning to be blessed with other foods. The breads are arrayed before the priest in baskets, each under the glow of its own lighted candle. It is richer than ordinary bread. Its central motif is a cross, sometimes made of twined or braided rolls. Other ornaments may be birds, fish and rosettes.

2 tablespoons yeast
2 tablespoons sugar
1 cup lukewarm water
3 cups milk scalded and cooled to lukewarm
5 cups flour
6 eggs beaten
1 cup sugar
½ cup melted butter
1 teaspoon salt
Enough flour to make soft dough (9-10 cups)

Dissolve sugar and yeast in water. Let stand 10 minutes. Add yeast mixture to milk and 5 cups of flour. Beat well, cover and let stand in warm place for an hour until light and bubbly. Add eggs, sugar, salt and butter, mixing thoroughly. Now, start adding sifted flour a little at a time until you have a dough you can knead. Knead until smooth. Place in bowl, cover and let rise until doubled. Punch down and let rise again. Divide dough in three parts.

Form round loaves to fill 2 buttered pans and save third part of dough for making decorations. Pans should be 3 to 4 inches deep.

Divide reserve dough in two to make ornaments. The big ornament is a cross. You can make this with two rolls of dough, simply crossed, tucking ends under the loaf. Fill in the arms of the cross with swirls or rosettes, using a sharp scissors to snip petals on the rosettes. Place a round flat piece of dough, snipped in 7 places, over center of cross.

Some make a stiffer dough to assure doughs will hold their shape in rising and baking. And some make elaborate crosses with twined or braided rolls, and make birds to fill in the arms.

Place decorations on the loaf when it is half risen. When it is ready for the oven, brush with egg and water mix – 1 egg to 2 tablespoons of water.

Bake at 400° for 15 minutes, lower heat to 350° and continue baking another 40 minutes. If tops begin to brown too much, make a cap of aluminum foil and finish baking.

Yield: 2 loaves

NO KNEAD RUSSIAN EASTER BREAD

When a Russian family offers you a slice of Kulich, or better yet, a half loaf, they care enough to give you the very best. With Kulich comes the hidden gift: hours of work and preparation. Here is a beautifully simple version.

KULICH

7½ cups flour
1 cup brown sugar
1 cup butter
1 cup currants
¼ cup almonds
2 tablespoons yeast
1½ cups milk, scalded and cooled to lukewarm
5 eggs
½ teaspoon vanilla
½ teaspoon saffron
Pinch of salt
1/3 cup candied peel or glacé cherries

Make batter with half the flour and the yeast dissolved in warm milk. Cover and leave in a warm place to rise.

Cream butter and sugar. Mix in yolks of 4 eggs, salt, vanilla, saffron and remaining flour. (We sift salt and saffron with flour in order to distribute it evenly. Otherwise saffron tends to clot.) Add to yeast batter. Fold in 5 egg whites beaten stiff. Put in warm place to rise again.

Chop candied peel and almonds, wash and dry currants and add to dough mixing well.

Kulich is traditionally baked in tall, round tins. For this recipe we used 2-pound coffee cans. Butter them inside and sprinkle with flour, shaking to make an even film. Line the bottoms with waxed paper or a piece of cardboard covered with waxed paper.

Fill half way up with dough, cover with a cloth and put in a warm place to rise ¾ the way up. Brush tops with remaining egg yolk and bake at 350° for an hour.

Dough will rise over top during baking. To prevent further browning after tops are golden brown, cover with damp waxed paper. When bread is done, remove from cans at once and cool on racks. When bread has cooled, ice tops with lemon glaze and decorate with cherries or candied peel.

Yield: 2 loaves

LEMON GLAZE

3 tablespoons softened butter
1 egg yolk
Grated rind of a lemon
2 tablespoons lemon juice
2 cups sifted powdered sugar

Blend butter, yolk, lemon rind and juice until smooth. Add sugar and stir until smooth. Allow glaze to dribble over sides in long tongues. You will have glaze left over for an angel food cake, in case the mood strikes you. Glaze keeps well.

Kulich keeps very well in the freezer. So you can make it well ahead of time. Serve in sliced rounds, keeping the bottom crust as a protective cover to prevent the loaf from drying out. A whole loaf makes a beautiful and memorable gift for a friend.

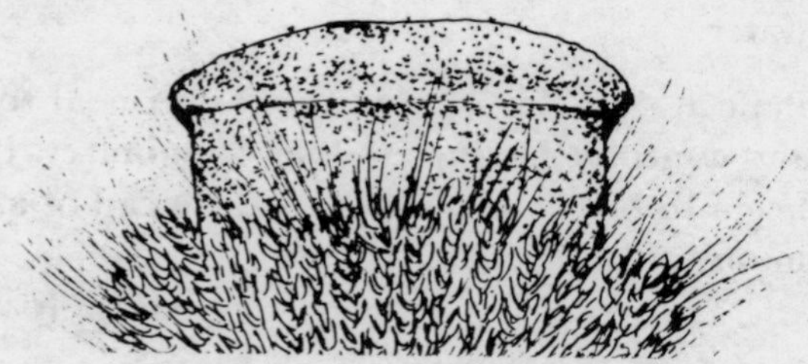

AN ICELANDIC CHRISTMAS BREAD

This is Lil Austman's recipe from Winnipeg and if it were not in loaf form, it would do very well as a formula for some Norwegian rolls served every Sunday morning in the college dining room at Minnesota. We got up early to get our share on winter mornings and our Chinese friends at school gave us theirs in exchange for any rice that might be served any time during the week!

JOLA BRAUD

1 tablespoon yeast
1 cup milk, scalded and cooled
1 tablespoon sugar
3 1/4 cups sifted flour
1/4 cup butter
1 cup sugar
1 egg well beaten
1/4 teaspoon salt
1/2 cup raisins
1/2 cup candied peel
3 drops oil of lemon
1/8 teaspoon crushed cardamom

Dissolve yeast and tablespoon of sugar in milk. Add 1½ cups flour to make batter. Beat until smooth. Cover and let rise in warm place until light, about 1 hour.

Cream butter and sugar. Add egg, raisins, peel, spice and flavoring. Add to yeast batter. Add remaining flour sifted with salt to make stiff dough. Turn out on board and knead lightly. Place in buttered bowl, cover and allow to rise until double in bulk, about 2 hours.

Put in buttered bread pan and let rise again for another hour. Glaze with egg diluted with water just before baking. Bake at 350°. Just before bread is done, brush with sugar moistened with water.

Yield: 1 loaf

A BREAD THAT IS A CHRISTCHILD IN SWADDLING CLOTHES

The Germans make an elaborate, frosted bread called Stollen for Christmas. For us, it has been the ultimate gift at Yuletide from a thoughtful Chinese friend.

One of the easiest ways to make Stollen is to fly to Germany!

Just as in medieval times, housewives there take breads to their favorite bakers to be finished. Contemporaries do so because the small apartment-size ovens don't allow housewives to consider doing much baking at home.

In the small town of Ladenburg, Germany, just seven miles from Heidelberg where our niece, Judy Parsons grew up, there are seven bakers.

"We would mix two or three loaves of bread at home," she told us, "and let them rise. Then we covered the breads with a towel or tablecloth and took them to our favorite baker. He marked the pans to identify each customer, baked the loaves, cooled the finished bread and even wrapped it in waxed paper for us.

"At Christmastime when we were rushed, we could measure out the raw ingredients – so much sugar, butter, flour and so on – for cookies or Stollen. The baker mixed it all for us. He would even make four or five different kinds of cookies from the ingredients. He would bake anything we wanted."

And so it is today. Since you are not likely to fly to Germany to have your Stollen baked, here is how you can accomplish it alone.

STOLLEN

2/3 cup lukewarm water
3 teaspoons sugar
3 tablespoons yeast
1 1/2 cups milk scalded
2/3 cup sugar
1/2 cup soft butter
3 eggs, beaten
1/2 cup sherry
4 cups flour sifted with
2 teaspoons salt
1 cup seedless raisins
1 cup currants
2 cups candied peel
1 cup chopped walnuts
Grated rinds of 1 lemon and 1 orange
Enough extra flour to make good dough – 3 or 4 cups

Combine water, sugar and yeast and let foam. Scald milk, remove from heat and cool to lukewarm and add to yeast mix.

In a large bowl cream sugar and butter thoroughly. Add beaten eggs and sherry, mixing well, and then add yeast mix. Stir in flour and mix thoroughly. Work in fruits and nuts and grated rind, dusted with a little flour.

Add remaining flour and turn out on board. Knead until smooth. Let rise in buttered, covered bowl until double in bulk. Punch down and divide into 2 or 3 pieces. Form oval shapes and fold not quite in half lengthwise to create traditional Stollen shape. Let rise again on buttered baking sheets until about double in size.

Bake at 350° for 1 hour. If loaves seem to be browning too fast, cover with a cap of aluminum foil and continue baking.

When breads are done, brush with butter. When they have cooled, brush again with butter and sprinkle lavishly with icing sugar.

Keep the loaves for several days to improve cutting quality. Slice thin and serve with sweet butter.

Yield: 2 or 3 Stollens

SO THIS WONDERFUL THING IS WHAT "THEY" EAT!

What an adventure in human diversity it is to make feast breads that originate in a far away land and alien culture! Each one brings you a step closer to understanding someone else's beautiful style.

Every national group has special breads with special shapes and we don't know of a one that it isn't fun to try . . . Greek Vasilopeta, Jewish Challah, Italian Panettone and Cresca, Finnish Pulla, Norwegian Julekaka, Austrian Gugelhupf and Striezel, Swedish Lussekatter, Czechoslovakian Vánočká and Babovka, Russian Babka, Argentinian Pan Paraiso, Danish Fastelavnsholler, Mexican Rosca de Reyes, Irish Barmbrack, French Gâteau des Rois.

Some are quite alike with just enough accent to make them delightfully individual.

THE GREAT HAMBURGER BUN HUNT

America's No. 1 eat-out favorite is the hamburger. With billions of hamburgers being sold every year, you would think there would be more attention paid to home made hamburger buns than there has been.

This is a field wide open for your exploration and invention.

NOT ON BUNS ALONE, OF COURSE

It is true that not all hamburgers come to table served on big round buns. Many kinds of sliced breads perform. A featured favorite at a number of San Francisco's restaurant is the famous San Francisco Sour Dough French Bread.

At Original Joe's, the long French loaves are cut off in seven-inch chunks. The soft inner bread is stripped from the crust to hollow out a place for the hamburger. At Hippo's, round loaves of sour dough French bread are sliced to give the customer a cross section of crust and bread.

MANY BREADS QUALIFY FOR THE HONOR

Just about any kind of good bread can be designed as a hamburger bun. We have already noted what a good thing the Arabian flat bread is as a hamburger bun. It makes an excellent receptacle for a fill-it-yourself hamburger buffet.

Very often when we bake bread, we set aside part of the dough to shape big buns and bake them in stoneware oven proof cereal bowls. These bowls are 5 inches in diameter and 1½ inches deep — just the right size. This makes it possible to have a great variety of hamburger buns in the freezer.

We have had hamburger buns made with whole wheat, with sour rye, with many kinds of white. Some are plain, some are made with cheese in them. Some are sprinkled with poppy seeds or sesame and some with oat flakes. Some are Cornellized with dry milk solids, wheat germ and soy flour, just to make the meal in a bun really nutritious.

ABSOLUTELY THE GREATEST!

Not so long ago, a tasting team from *The Canadian Magazine* set forth on the admirable quest to discover Canada's "absolutely greatest hamburger."

During their epic 10,891 mile journey from St. John's to Victoria to check out 11 finalists, the judges were especially impressed with a hamburger bun made from a recipe for Jewish Challah.

Quite rightly, we think, the bun won equal time with the meat and assorted condiments.

How does one make this handsome braided egg bread perform as a bun?

ALL THE NEWS THAT'S FIT TO PRINT

A short time before the Canadians went on their hamburger safari, *The New York Times* announced "Challah Expert Tells All." The two events were simply coincidental.

The Challah expert was a Mrs. Hollander, 82. She had been making Challah for 57 years and baking it in the same pans every Friday. She confessed that she was never given to measuring. "I looked in the bowl and knew what to do." And when she finished the breads, she put them near an open window to make the outside especially crusty. She advised that the right attitute is as important as the right ingredients.

CHALLAH

6 cups unsifted unbleached flour
2 tablespoons yeast
1 1/3 cups lukewarm water
1 tablespoon sugar
3/4 tablespoon coarse salt
3 tablespoons corn oil
3 large eggs, beaten

Sift flour into large mixing bowl. Into 2/3 cup of the warm water, sprinkle the yeast, and mix well. Pour this into a little well you have made in the sifted flour.

Combine sugar, salt, oil and remaining warm water in a large heatproof glass measuring cup and mix well. Place in a sauce pan filled with warm water over low heat. When mixture is lukewarm, add eggs, reserving 1 tablespoon of egg for brushing tops of buns. Mrs. Hollander keeps stirring this mixture until it is smooth and like a custard, but she doesn't let the stuff get too hot.

Now add the egg mixture to the flour and yeast in the mixing bowl and stir until it makes a soft ball.

Knead the dough right in the mixing bowl, digging in with both hands. "Knead away for dear life, up and around, down and outwards. Pat it gently and say a prayer," advised Mrs. Hollander.

Let rise after you have oiled the surface and covered with a towel. This takes about 1 hour. Punch dough down and knead gently for a few minutes.

At this point, you part company with Mrs. Hollander.

She makes braids for the traditional Challah. You can start here to make the hamburger bun that conquered Canada.

Roll dough out 1/4 inch thick and cut with a 3 1/2-inch biscuit cutter. Place rounds on buttered cookie sheet 3 to 4 inches apart, cover and let rise until nearly double in bulk. Brush tops with remaining egg. Bake at 400° for about 20-25 minutes.

Yield: 2 dozen buns

AN HERBAN BUN

Making hamburger buns can set the stage for every conceivable combination of herbs – fresh or dried – depending strictly on personal taste. Here is an especially good reason for playing the New Entity Bread Game. Use the following bun recipe as a point of departure

SAVORY HAMBURGER BUNS

½ cup milk ¼ cup butter 1 tablespoon sugar 1½ teaspoon salt	Scald milk and add butter, sugar and salt. Cool to lukewarm.
1 teaspoon sugar ½ cup lukewarm water 1 tablespoon yeast	Combine and allow yeast to foam up, about 10 minutes. Add to cooled milk mixture.
1 lightly beaten egg ¼ teaspoon savory ½ teaspoon onion salt ½ teaspoon celery seeds 3 cups flour	Blend into liquids and mix well. Dough should be stiff enough to handle. Turn out on bread board and knead until smooth.

Set to rise in buttered, covered bowl. Refrigerate for 2 hours. Roll out ¼ inch thick, cut with 3½-inch biscuit cutter, place on buttered cookie sheet about 3 or 4 inches apart, cover and let rise until double in bulk, about 1 hour. Bake at 400° 20-25 minutes.

Yield: 14 buns

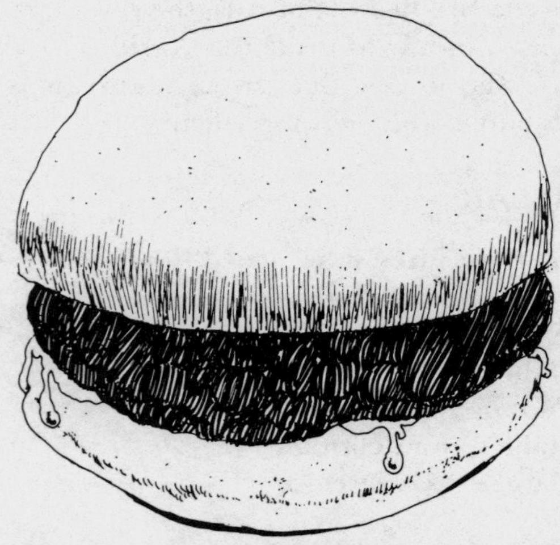

SOMETHING LIGHTLY FANTASTIC

If you have ever dreamed of having a hamburger that floats in on a wispy bun it can overwhelm, give some thought to "air buns."

The easiest way to enjoy them is to have a visiting grandmother from Rose Valley who will improve the shining hours – as we have heard one does – baking up batches for freezers wherever she goes!

AIR BUNS

½ cup lukewarm water
1 teaspoon sugar
1 tablespoon yeast

½ cup sugar
½ cup shortening

1 teaspoon salt
2 tablespoons vinegar
3½ cups warm water

Mix first 3 ingredients and let stand for 10 minutes. In a large bowl mix remaining ingredients, add yeast mix and enough flour to keep dough from being sticky – about 8 – 10 cups. Let rise in warm place in buttered, covered bowl for 2 hours. Knead down, let rise another hour. Knead down again. Form balls and set wide apart on buttered cookie sheets as they rise a great deal. Cover with cloth and allow to rise another 3 hours. Bake at 400° until golden brown. Brush with butter and cool on wire racks.

Yield: 5 dozen buns

BUILD THE CHEESE RIGHT IN

If your favorite is a cheeseburger, you may enjoy cheese buns with your hamburger. Here is one way to make them.

CHEDDAR CHEESE BUNS

1 tablespoon yeast
¼ cup warm water
2 cups milk scalded
¼ cup butter
1 teaspoon salt
½ cup sugar
1 egg beaten
5 – 6 cups flour
2 cups grated cheddar cheese (½ pound)
Melted butter

Combine water and yeast and let foam. Pour scalded milk into mixing bowl and add sugar, butter and salt. Cool to lukewarm and add egg and yeast mix. Add 2 cups flour and mix well, gradually stirring in remaining flour to make soft dough. Add cheese with last cups. Turn out on floured board and knead until satiny. Put in buttered bowl, brush with butter, cover and let rise until double in bulk in warm place. Punch down. Let rest.

Roll out dough as for Challah and Savory Buns, cut rounds with biscuit cutter and place on buttered cookie sheets and let rise until double in bulk. Bake in 375° oven 20-25 minutes.

Yield: 2 dozen buns

WHEN A BREAD BECOMES A CAKE

If elaborately decorated Ukrainian breads are the work of epic poets, cake breads must be the province of the lyric poets. They are quick. They admit gracefully to hundreds of flights of fancy. You can quickly learn a recipe and forever after let your imagination soar.

Here are the breads that let you play bountiful host even if guests arrive and your bread box is empty. They are very soon on the table. And contrary to common notions, you don't have to be sweet about them. You can make wonderful cake breads with herbs. You can "Cornellize" them for the sake of nutrition. You can experiment with flours, seasonings, flavorings, nuts, seeds and other bread stuffs. And you can taste the results in jig time.

What is more you can defy old wives' tales and eat them hot, if you like.

In the hands of the creative baker, the recipe is only the starting point. The only sure way to tap her talent is to follow her around and see what she does and ask, "Why are you doing that?"

She will generously share her creations without ever telling her secrets. This is not because she wants to keep her excellence to herself. She simply – after numerous trials and tests – adapts and adopts what she wants and becomes automatic. She does dozens of things she never thinks to tell you when she hands over the written recipe.

Suppose you watch the making of an Irish Soda Bread. There is the recipe, for a reminder, but many other things are going on. The baker likes the taste of soy flour; so she revises the recipe and substitutes some soy for some regular flour and throws in a little wheat germ. In the middle of the mixing, she disappears into her garden and comes back with sprigs of fresh oregano and thyme. "How much?" you ask. "What I think will be enough!" If these six 3-inch sprigs aren't enough, I'll try again some day and add more."

"Why these herbs?" you ask. "Because I like tea made with them."

THE JOY OF MIXING

When the baker gets around to buttering a round pan for the little round loaf that is developing, she butters her hands at the same time. Now she goes back to the mixing bowl, lifts out the ball of lightly mixed stuff and shapes it with her bare hands.

Why? "Well this keeps me from stirring the life out of the dough. I pat it into place and add a little butter in the process. I suppose it enriches the loaf, but mostly it's a maneuver to 'gentle' the dough and keep it tender. Besides, it's fun!"

ALL IN NINETY MINUTES OR LESS

So there's the little round loaf in the pan. You cut a cross on top to scare the devil away, pop the loaf into the oven and 30 minutes later – more or less – you have a beautiful, fragrant loaf and guests applaud from the living room!

A "MOTHER" RECIPE

Here is a soda bread formula that makes a good "mother" recipe. Made just as the recipe directs, it provides a bread of excellent edibility. As a "mother" recipe, it lets you dream up dozens of offspring.

IRISH SODA BREAD

- 2 cups flour
- 1/3 cup sugar
- 1/2 teaspoon salt
- 1 1/2 teaspoons baking powder
- 1/2 teaspoon soda
- 3/4 cup raisins
- 1 teaspoon caraway seeds
- 1 lightly beaten egg
- 2/3 cup buttermilk
- 1 tablespoon melted butter

Sift together flour, sugar, salt, baking powder and soda into bowl. Add raisins and caraway. In separate bowl beat egg and add buttermilk and butter. Stir into dry ingredients just enough to moisten throughout. If dough is still too sticky to handle lightly, add a little flour. Knead lightly with your hands and shape into a plump disk. Cut a cross on top and it's ready to go onto a buttered pan and into a 350° oven to bake for 30 – 35 minutes.

Cool a little on a wire rack, cut in thin slices and serve warm with butter.

Yield: 1 8-inch loaf

JUST REMOVE THE RAISINS AND CARAWAY . . . .

Raisins and caraway give this soda bread its distinctive taste. Just remove them and your mother recipe has a vast potential for variations.

You can go Russian if you own some saffron and feel you can afford to introduce it to soda bread along with a bit of brandy.

Or be Italian, Panettone style, and bring into the recipe grated lemon rind, aniseed, candied fruit, pine nuts and an extra egg yolk.

Go Early American and use half whole wheat and half white flour and use dried herbs. This will satisfy your hunger right down to your toes!

Perhaps something a little Czechoslovakian would hit the spot. Use lemon rind and juice, almonds and poppyseeds.

Maybe you are hungry for Norwegian Julekaka some cold winter day. Restore the raisins and add citron and cardamom.

Or just be you and invent something from what you have in the kitchen, on the spice shelves or in the refrigerator. Be adventurous.

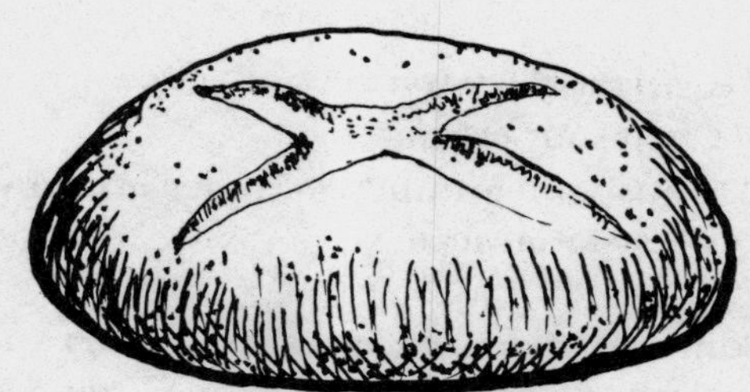

THE LITTLE BREAD THAT IS ALWAYS THERE

No matter how many interesting yeast breads we have made, we always come back to the soda breads. One of its versions we have repeated again and again. Here it is. We use powdered or dry herbs.

EARLY AMERICAN HERB BREAD

- 1 cup whole wheat
- 2/3 cup white
- 1/3 cup soy flour
- 2 tablespoons sugar
- 1/2 teaspoon salt
- 1 1/2 teaspoons baking powder
- 1/2 teaspoon soda
- 1/4 teaspoon marjoram
- 1/4 teaspoon oregano
- 1/2 teaspoon basil
- Pinch of thyme
- 1 egg lightly beaten
- 2/3 cup buttermilk
- 1 tablespoon low fat salad oil

Sift all dry ingredients together, including herbs, into bowl and follow instructions above for soda bread.

Serve warm with sweet butter and a glass of cold milk.

THE SHOW OFFS

There is always the day you say, "This bread I am going to make is going to be *beautiful*!" Again, soda bread and the mother recipe to the rescue. You can make

CITRON BREAD

This makes a good, crusty, but delicate loaf. It slices to yellow flecked with the pale green of citron. It is delicious with thin slices of cheddar and other cheese – or simply with sweet butter and cold milk. It does not keep well – simply because it doesn't last all that long!

- 1¾ cups flour
- ½ cup soy flour
- 1 heaping tablespoon wheat germ
- 1½ teaspoons baking powder
- ½ teaspoon soda
- 3 egg yolks
- ½ cup buttermilk
- 1 tablespoon melted butter
- ½ cup coarsely chopped citron

Sift flours together with baking powder and soda into a bowl and stir in wheat germ thoroughly. In a separate bowl beat egg yolks well and add buttermilk and butter. Fold into dry ingredients and carry on!

WHAT ABOUT THAT ALMOND PASTE IN THE REFRIGERATOR?

It was not only almond paste but also an urgency to make use of sour cream and sweet rice flour that brought on the next bread. Its making also provided a joyous experience with surface decorations on the loaf.

ALMOND BREAD

In a measuring cup, measure out
1/2 cup sweet rice flour
1 tablespoon wheat germ
Complete filling of cup with white flour
Add 1 cup more of white flour, sifted with
1/4 cup sugar
1/2 teaspoon salt
1 1/2 teaspoons baking powder
1/2 teaspoon soda
2 tablespoons almond paste
1 egg lightly beaten
1/2 cup sour cream
1/3 teaspoon ground coriander mixed with
1/3 teaspoon sugar

Combine measured and sifted flours and blend in almond paste with your fingers as for pie crust. Work the stuff until almond paste is reduced to small granules. Add lightly beaten egg and sour cream. Knead very lightly. Instead of cutting a cross on top, crosshatch lightly and sprinkle with coriander and sugar mix.

This comes out of the oven looking like a big, golden sugarplum. Like a little girl we once knew who wanted to keep forever the first little fish she caught, we found it hard to give up this bread with its beautiful top!

MORE CAKE THAN BREAD

There comes a time when a bread may be a cake parading in disguise, like the Royal Apple Bread. Its origin is Holland with a detour through the Northwest. It comes from Tina Troost's Uncle Jan who was once a baker in Holland.

Unlike soda breads which can be quite Spartan if you like, this cake bread is rich and sweet. And it is made the way many cakes are made. Eat it with some homely cheese or enjoy it toasted for Sunday breakfast. And after you have savored it, think of all the other kinds of nuts and grated fresh fruit you might try some time.

UNCLE JAN'S ROYAL APPLE BREAD

2/3 cup shortening
1 1/3 cups sugar
4 eggs
1/3 cup sour milk or buttermilk
2 cups peeled, grated apple
4 cups flour
2 teaspoons baking powder
1 teaspoon salt
1 teaspoon soda
1 teaspoon cinnamon
1/4 teaspoon mace
1 cup chopped walnuts

Cream shortening with sugar. Add eggs and beat well. Stir in sour milk and apples. Sift dry ingredients together and stir in. Add nuts. Pour into 2 buttered loaf pans. Let stand 20 minutes. Bake at 350° for 50-60 minutes. Turn out and cool on rack.

MIX NOW

You can break the breadcraft cycle.

If you are interrupted when you are beating or kneading dough, you can stop for 15 minutes or more. Merely cover your dough to keep it from drying out. It will be even easier to handle when you return.

If dough has risen twice, punch it down and let it rise again, if you are not ready. If it rises too much in the pan before going into the oven, take it out and knead it again, reshape it and let it rise once more.

If something calls you away, don't worry, your refrigerator and its freezing compartment will save your dough. If you don't like being tied down over a period of hours, you have an out: you can mix now and bake later.

Since yeast is a living organism and thrives on temperatures between 70° and 90°F., lesser temperatures will retard it. The dough, in other words, can be laid to rest and rise again at your convenience.

FREEZE ACTION OPTION

You can freeze bread dough for periods up to two weeks. After that the leavening power of the yeast decreases. When you are ready to resume the breadcrafting cycle, you can thaw the dough in three hours at room temperature or overnight in the refrigerator. Just pick up the recipe directions and carry on from the point at which you set the dough aside.

& BAKE LATER BREADS

When you freeze dough, wrap it in foil or plastic. Remember that dough will expand somewhat before it freezes. Shape the dough into loaves smaller than the pans you plan to bake them in and find a flat surface for them in the freezer.

This means you can bake as much of a recipe as you like and freeze the remainder to bake later.

DELAYED ACTION OPTION

If you just want to put off baking for a day or two, you can mix now and bake later when you are ready or have more time. Simply refrigerate, without freezing. When you are ready to bake, remove the dough from the refrigerator, let it stand 10 minutes or so while you are preheating the oven. Most recipes will suggest you puncture any surface bubbles with an oiled toothpick before baking.

Doughs in Waiting

COOLRISE BREAD

Many recipes fall under the description of coolrise. Possible introductions to this basic white version are raisins, cheese-caraway, cheese-onion-bacon, herbs and orange-sesame. The dough makes excellent hamburger buns.

COOLRISE BREAD

2 teaspoons sugar
½ cup warm water
2 tablespoons yeast
5½ - 6½ cups flour
(Of this total amount we include ¼ cup each of wheat germ and soy flour)
1¾ cups warm milk
2 tablespoons sugar
1 teaspoon salt
3 tablespoons shortening
Cooking oil

Dissolve sugar in warm water in large warm bowl and sprinkle yeast over it. Let stand 10 minutes.

Measure out flour onto wax paper, stirring in soy and wheat germ until they are well distributed.

Stir warm milk, sugar, salt and shortening into yeast mixture. Add 2 cups of flour and beat with a rotary beater or electric hand mixer until smooth. Add another cup of flour and beat vigorously with a wooden spoon – about 150 strokes.

(NOTE: This is the point at which you can introduce variations, for example, 2 cups of raisins; or a cup of grated cheese and 2 teaspoons of caraway seeds, etc. Then carry on with the recipe.)
Gradually stir in remaining flour until dough begins to pull away from sides of bowl. Turn out onto bread board and knead 5 to 10 minutes until dough is smooth and no longer sticky. Put in buttered bowl, cover and let rest for 20 minutes. Punch down.

Divide dough in two and shape into loaves or hamburger buns. Loaves should be oiled and placed in regular size buttered pans. Buns can be placed on buttered cookie sheet. Cover pans with oiled wax paper and then with plastic wrap. Place in refrigerator from 2 to 24 hours.

When you are ready to bake, remove from refrigerator and let stand at room temperature while you preheat your oven. Prick any bubbles that have formed on dough with an oiled toothpick or skewer.

Bake in 400° oven 30 - 40 minutes on lower rack. Remove from pans at once and brush crust with butter, if you like.

Yield: 2 regular loaves or
10 - 12 hamburger buns

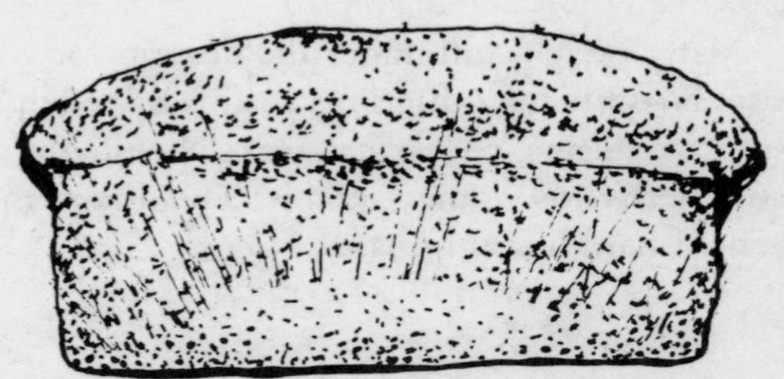

A PEARL AMONG BREADS

The Spanish discovered potatoes in the Andes in 1534. Some 200 years later a French apothecary named Parmentier set out to popularize them. His big chance came with a contest in Besançon where the quest was on to find a plant that would substitute for grains in time of famine. Parmentier's potato led all the rest and he set out to travel France, study bread and promote the potato as a source of flour for bread.

His all-potato bread failed. He obviously never enjoyed this pearl of a bread you are about to make. It is rich fare and worthy of the pampered swans of Bruges where bakers daily bake bread for them and have the town firemen deliver it to them on bicycles.

The dough is pleasant to handle and easy to manage after refrigeration. The dough will keep for a week under refrigeration. You will want to bake this bread many times.

MASHED POTATO BREAD

1 heaping tablespoon yeast
½ cup warm water
2/3 cup butter
½ cup sugar
1 teaspoon salt
1 cup hot mashed potatoes
1 cup scalded milk
2 eggs well beaten
Flour to make a good sponge – 5 ~ 6 cups

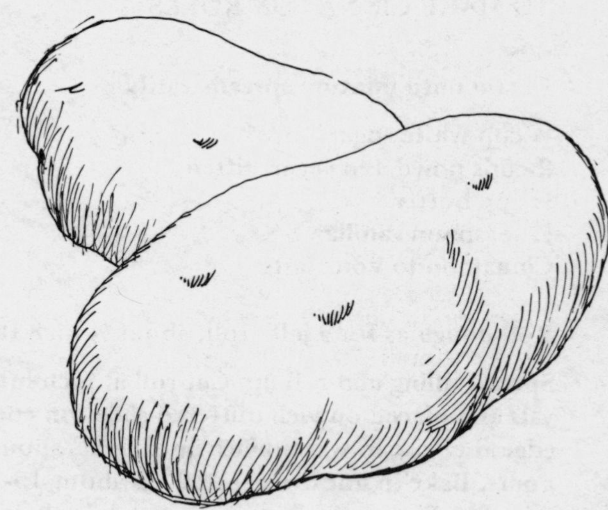

Dissolve yeast in water. Let stand. Combine butter, sugar, salt and hot mashed potatoes with scalded milk and cool to lukewarm. Add yeast mix. Blend thoroughly and add eggs and enough flour to make a stiff dough.

Turn out on floured board and knead for about 10 minutes. Place in buttered bowl, cover and refrigerate over night or until you are ready to use it.

To bake, shape and let rise once until double in bulk. Bake at 400° for 20 minutes, then at 300° for 30 minutes.

Yield: 2 loaves or
1 loaf and
a dozen cinnamon rolls

TO MAKE CINNAMON ROLLS

Cream until mixture spreads easily:

¼ cup white sugar
2 cups powdered sugar, sifted
½ cup butter
½ teaspoon vanilla
Cinnamon to your taste

Roll dough as for a jelly roll, about ¼ inch thick.

Spread filling and roll up. Cut roll at inch intervals and placed on well buttered sheet on cut edge. Let rise in warm place until light, about 2 hours. Bake in hot oven – 400° – about 15-20 minutes. Remove rolls from pans while they are still warm. Otherwise the sugar will carmelize and the rolls will resist everything but brute force and look the worse for your struggle.

If you fancy making these into toppleover buns, put them in a buttered 8-inch square pan and fit them in tightly enough to force the dough up and topple over.

The beauty of this recipe is that you can make bread one day and have unforgettable cinnamon rolls the next. If over night guests are in the offing, what a wonderful way this is to perform near miracles at dinner one night and at breakfast the next day. The recipe is also adaptable to dinner rolls.

Rolls and Buns

ICE BOX ROLLS

When you get ready to bake these rolls, you can shape the chilled dough and arrange the rolls in a square pan in a block, a dozen to a pan. You can hold the remaining dough in the refrigerator for another day.

2 cups milk scalded and cooled
1 tablespoon yeast
½ cup lukewarm water
½ teaspoon sugar
½ cup butter
½ cup sugar
1 beaten egg
½ teaspoon salt
Enough flour to make very soft dough, about 7 cups.

Scald milk. Mix and let stand: yeast and ½ teaspoon sugar in lukewarm water.

Cream sugar and butter and add egg and salt, yeast mixture and cooled milk. Stir in flour until you have a kneadable dough. Knead well and let rise until double in bulk. Knead once more and place in buttered bowl. Cover and store in refrigerator until ready to bake.

To make one dozen rolls, use 1/3 of the dough. Form into rolls and put into buttered pan to rise – about 1½ to 2 hours for chilled dough. Bake in moderate oven 15 minutes.

Total yield: 3 dozen

NO KNEAD BUNS

Once mixed and refrigerated, these buns are ready. The dough will keep for a week in the refrigerator.

Mix and allow to cool until lukewarm:

2 cups boiling water
½ cup sugar
1 teaspoon salt
2 tablespoons butter

Combine and add to first mixture

¼ cup lukewarm water
2 tablespoons yeast
1 tablespoon sugar

Stir in:

2 well beaten eggs
4 or 5 cups sifted flour

Beat thoroughly. Place in a covered bowl and refrigerate 2 days or more before using.

When ready to use, form buns and place in well buttered muffin tins to rise – about 3 hours. Bake in moderate oven 12 - 15 minutes. Serve at once.

Yield: 3 dozen

BRIOCHE, BEAUTIFUL BRIOCHE!

Rich in butter and eggs, the elegant brioche was once considered an aristocratic appurtenance. Crisply crusty outside and delectably soft inside, they can be started one day, refrigerated over night and shaped and baked the next day or the next. They are, in fact, to be preferred when the dough has aged a bit.

You can let your electric mixer or portable hand beater do the hard work. And you can make handsome brioche without benefit of the traditional fluted pans. We have baked them in stoneware dessert bowls. So don't let lack of pans stop you. You will, however, feel very rewarded and rejoice noisily if you see your rolls come out of the oven gracefully shaped in the Continental manner.

BRIOCHE

¾ cup milk scalded and cooled to lukewarm
2 tablespoons sugar
1 teaspoon salt
2 tablespoons yeast
¼ cup warm water
5 cups unsifted flour
1 cup softened butter
5 eggs

Scald milk and add sugar and salt and cool. Dissolve yeast in warm water. Combine yeast and milk mixtures in large bowl. Stir in 2 cups of flour and blend well. Add butter and continue beating. Stir in remaining flour alternately with eggs, one at a time. Beat thoroughly after each addition until you have a soft sticky dough.

If you are using an electric mixer, beat at medium speed until dough is shiny and elastic. This takes about 10 minutes. You may find that the dough is too heavy for your mixer after awhile.

Remove it to another bowl and continue mixing by hand until dough is no longer sticky.

Put the dough in a buttered bowl, cover and let rise in a warm place until double in bulk, about 1½ hours. Punch down, cover with plastic wrap and refrigerate over night.

To bake, fill well buttered brioche pans half full with a ball shaped piece of dough. Snip an X on top the dough with your kitchen scissors or a knife and press down where the cuts intersect and make a hole. Into this hole fit a teardrop shaped piece of dough about the size of a walnut. Set pans to rise in a warm place until double in size – about 2 hours. Brush tops with a glaze made of egg yolk and milk.

Preheat oven to 425° and bake brioche on rack placed below center of oven. Bake at 425° for 10 minutes, then reduce heat to 325° and bake another 15-18 minutes. This is for molds that measure 5½ inches in diameter.

If rolls brown too much, cover them with a sheet of aluminum foil and continue baking. Serve hot.

Yield: 12 brioches

A BATTER BREAKTHROUGH VIA TINA TROOST

Cache this muffin mix in your refrigerator. Here is a batter you can stash away and keep bringing out at strategic moments in various guises. The batter will keep in the refrigerator up to several weeks. You can bake as many or as few at a time as it suits you. We keep the batter in a big covered bean pot. As we spoon out what batter we want to use, we introduce the variations. These have included currants and chopped sunflower seeds; grated orange rind; grated lemon rind and caraway seeds; minced citron; grated fresh apple; chopped dried figs, apricots, dates or prunes; and crushed pineapple well drained.

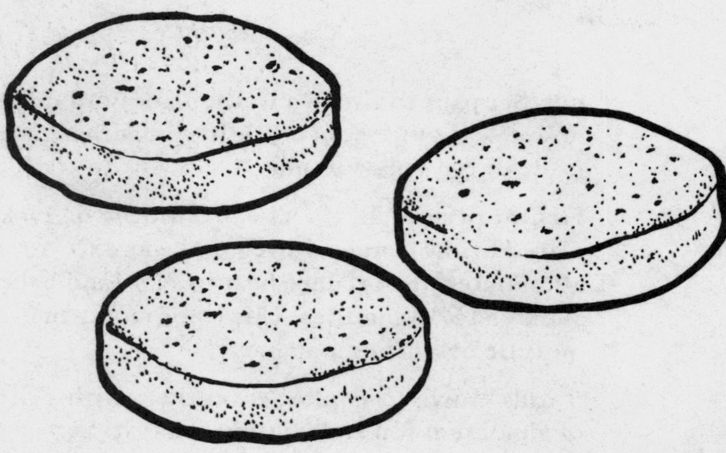

EVERLASTING MUFFINS

2 cups all-bran
1 cup boiling water
2½ cups flour
2½ teaspoons soda
2 teaspoons salt
½ cup + 1 tablespoon shortening
1½ cups sugar
2 eggs
2 cups buttermilk

Pour boiling water over bran and allow to stand 15 minutes. Sift flour, measure and add soda and salt. Cream shortening, blend in sugar and eggs. Beat until fluffy. Stir in bran. Add flour and buttermilk, alternately. Store batter in refrigerator and bake at convenience.

To bake, fill well buttered muffin tins about 2/3 full. Bake 20 - 25 minutes, depending on size of muffins. Bake at 400°.

Yield: 3 dozen

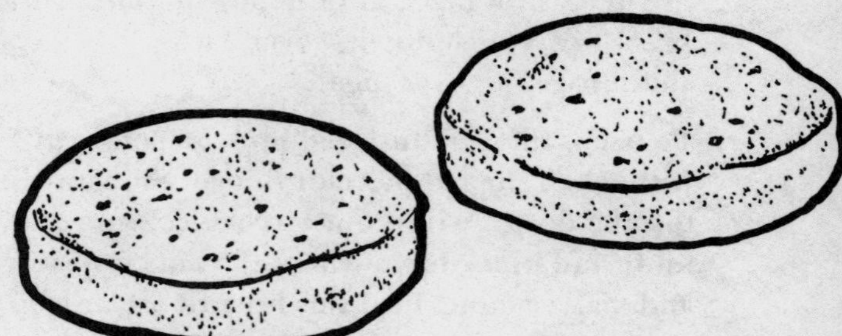

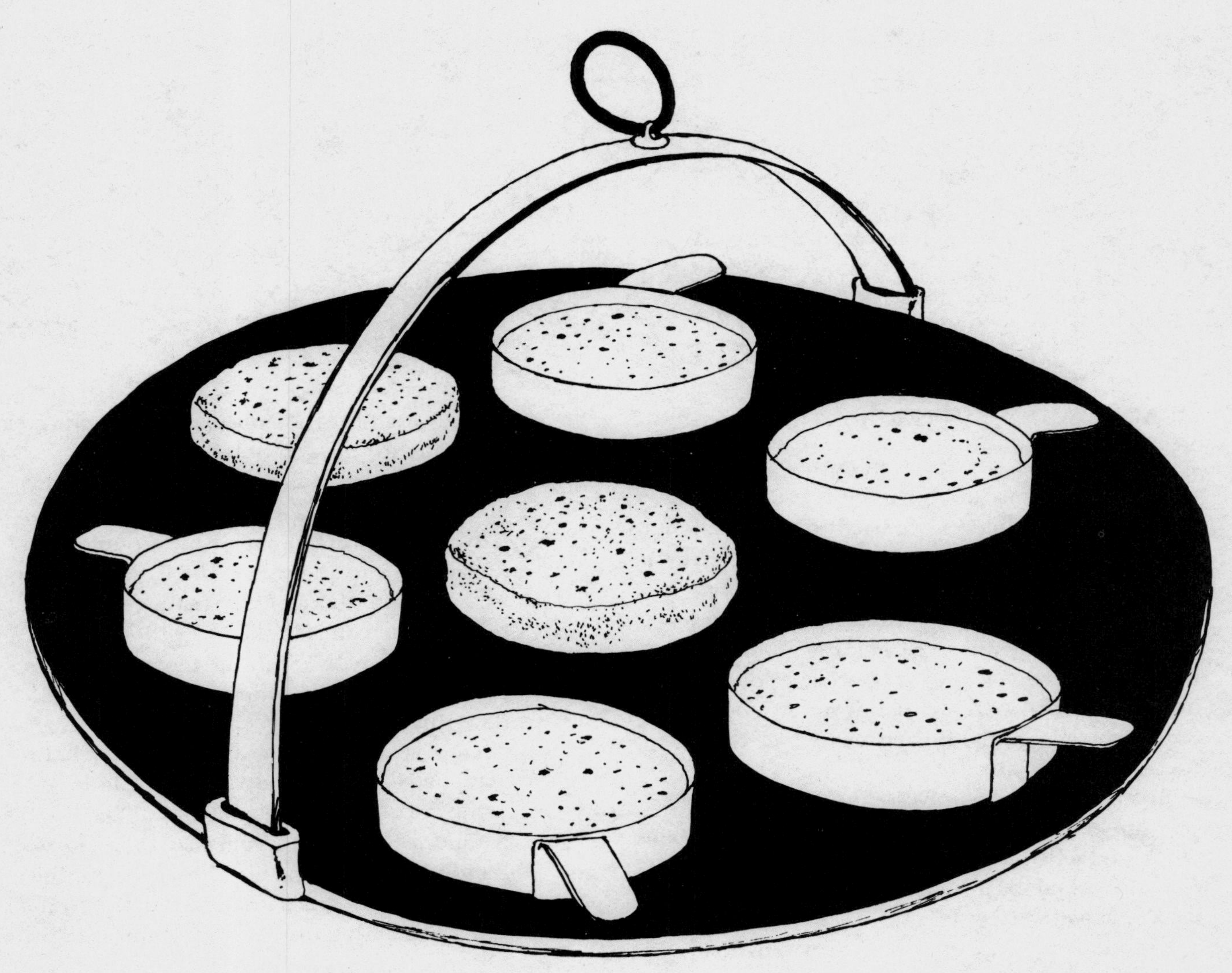

BREAD SPREADS – BUTTER, JAM & JELLIES

MEADOWS AND BUTTERCUPS

Springtime has always been meadowtime — a time of dandelions and buttercups and little things in the grass. As children we tried to pick the longest-stemmed dandelions to weave into wreaths. With them on our heads and tired from play, we sat in the grass and picked buttercups as divining rods. We held them under each other's chin. If the skin glowed yellow, we crowed, "You like butter!" Hardly a little chin but did not borrow butter color from the flower, yet we made the test again and again.

Butter was indeed universally favored and we grew up in a time when butter was sold in a pound block and when many of us still had grandmothers on farms where butter making was a home chore usually assigned to girls.

Grandmother had a special Jersey cow that was her "house cow." All the milk the Jersey produced was used for the house, including the cream she set aside for making butter.

Sister Spency cannot imagine now why she liked so much to make butter in that long ago.

"It was hard work. First I had to pump cold water to fill a tub and we set the earthenware churn in the tub to keep the cream cool as we worked it. The churn looked like those big umbrella stands you see in the movies. It had a wooden dasher with a paddle that fit snugly. I worked this up and down through a hole in a wooden cover that fit over the top of the churn. We wrapped a clean towel around the hole to keep the cream from splashing out.

"Grandma skimmed cream that formed on milk in big crocks in the well house. Sometimes the crocks were covered and put down into the well in a pail with a rope to haul it up and down.

This thick, sweet cream accumulated for several days or longer and ended in the churn and my long labor began — up and down, up and down!

"When the butter began to form, Grandma took the mass from the churn after pouring off the buttermilk with its little yellow flecks of butter. She washed it again and again with water from the well and kneaded the butter with her hands until the water ran clear. Then she salted the butter and stored it in a cool place."

A FAIRLY LONG HISTORY

In the United States butter was made on farms first. When there was more than the farm family needed, the butter makers gave their surplus to neighbors for cash or took it to village stores to exchange for other staples.

But who made the first butter in all the world? No one knows. It is presumed that butter making began during prehistoric stages of animal husbandry. Butter was known in the Middle East, in Egypt and parts of Northern Europe before the Greeks and Romans learned about it.

Classical butter was liquid. It was poured like oil. The ancients churned milk without separation, using bags made from animal skins.

Herodotus told of Scythian slaves who shook milk in deep wooden buckets and skimmed the butter off the surface. His contemporary Hippocrates noted that the Thracians and other northern peoples also made butter from milk. The geographer Strabo ascribed a taste for butter to the Iberians and Ethiopians.

Pliny who lived in the first century described butter as the most luxurious food of barbarous people. Butter was for the rich, and the ranker, the better!

In early times, butter was a part of religious rites and medicine. Hippocrates and Galen considered it a good unguent. Dioscorides prescribed it for inflamed eyes. He also suggested melting it and pouring it over porridge and vegetables.

Pliny described its usefulness in breadmaking, pointing out that in addition to eggs and milk, people in times of peace, used butter in making various kinds of pastry.

Actually olive oil, when it was available, was preferred to butter. Butter was seldom in demand except as medicine and in Mediterranean countries it was sold only in apothecary shops into the 17th Century.

In the North, butter was long an important food. As early as the 12th Century it was being exported in quantity from Scandinavia. Its popularity caused one of the towers of the Cathedral of Rouen to be called the "Butter Tower." It was built with money paid for indulgences permitting butter during Lent.

In the early 17th Century Icelanders built 30-foot chests of fir in which to store salted butter. These they buried in the ground for keeping.

When the 18th Century rolled around, butter was in copious use. A soup might require a pound of it. But it was not until refrigeration and rapid transport became common that good butter was in common use.

BUTTER'S AFFINITY FOR BREAD

Bread, because of its deficiency in fats, becomes a more perfect food when you spread butter on it. Reason enough for this preoccupation with butter.

The making of butter, like the making of sour dough breads incorporates starters. The flavor and aroma of butter result from a process of fermentation called "cream ripening." This occurs before cream is churned. The best flavor is obtained when cream assumes a clean, pure, acid taste during ripening. Since this is assisted by certain bacteria, butter makers have developed their own special starters and cultures.

A Missouri creamery, for example, uses a special Danish starter that gives its butter a sweet buttery taste that epitomizes butter. It fairly melts in your mouth.

Cream ripening is not essential to complete the churning process, but ripened cream will churn more easily than unripened cream. On farms butter makers depend on natural ripening, but this is a chancy matter since conditions favorable to ripening vary greatly during a year.

ONLY LOVE BEATS BUTTER (SIGN ON A TRUCK!)

The butter we buy is made from cow's milk, but there are other animals whose milk makes butter, particularly goats and sheep. The milk of all mammals contains fat. Churning breaks down the oil sacs, the liberated fat comes together and forms the butter. In Brittany they will tell you that the best butter is made when the tide has just turned.

Sans farm, sans cow and sans churn, you can make your own butter, provided you have a blender and some whipping cream. One cup will do.

BLENDER BUTTER

Put 1 cup heavy cream in blender. Blend at high speed for about 15 seconds. When cream has thickened around blades, pour in ½ cup very cold water with an ice cube and blend at high speed for 2 to 3 minutes. With spatula, push whipped cream down to blades. Add another ice cube if butter doesn't start to form. Butter will separate from liquid suddenly. Drain off water and knead butter with wooden spoon to extract all remaining liquid. Finish nicely with a butter paddle and refrigerate.

Yield: ¼ pound sweet butter

REGISTERED "EXTRA"

When you have made your own butter, you are entitled to play connoisseur and judge your performance. Experts score butter on body, flavor, color, salt and style. This is what they look for in each category:

Flavor— Sweet, clean, fresh. Butter should have a mild, rich, creamy taste and have a delicate, pleasant aroma — never be flat, rancid, cheesy, weedy or acid.

Body — Firm, smooth and uniform — not greasy, tallowy, spongy or sticky.

Color — Light straw shade, even and uniform, almost transparently bright; not cloudy, streaky or mottled.

Salt — Medium. If you are going to use salt at all, it must be thoroughly dissolved and evenly distributed.

Style — Neatly — and even attractively — finished.

If you score high on all counts, you have an Extra grade of butter, the finest. It will make that bread you have made a more perfect food, a more delicious meal.

NEVER, NEVER IN THE AIR!

Putting bread and butter together was the subject for that pillar of politeness, Emily Post. In an early edition of *Etiquette*, she suggested: Always break bread into small pieces before eating it. When you butter it (at lunch, breakfast, or supper, but not at dinner), hold a piece on the edge of the bread and butter plate, or placeplate, and spread on it enough butter for a mouthful or two at a time with a small silver "butter knife." Never, never hold a piece of bread flat on the palm of your hand and butter it in the air. She went on to deplore messiness and it is obvious, no one ever served French bread at her table.

SERVING BREAD AND BUTTER

The bread you bake and the butter you make deserve the best. Present them to please the eye as well as the appetite. Bring out the old silver, lovely old baskets, handsome bread boards and whitest linens. Light the candles and bring your bread and butter on stage.

One of the finest compliments we ever had came when we brought fresh herb breads to a gathering along with an armful of blossoming mint. The host sliced the breads, arranged the buttered pieces on long trays and laid the long stemmed mint between rows of bread. The simple gift of good fresh bread suddenly took on an importance in the menu and we felt richly rewarded. What was simply good became simply beautiful.

BUTTER BEGETS BUTTER

By its very nature, butter is a good mixer. You can make of it what you will, adding everything from lemon juice and dry mustard to chutney and curry powder.

To ¼ cup of butter you can add:
Chopped herbs, singly or in bouquet
Minced water cress
Grated cheese
Horseradish
Minced olives
You can mix equal parts of butter and honey.

And all of these go well on bread for sandwiches and on toast and biscuits. Here are two spreads that are very easy to make. The Lemon Butter is variously styled Lemon Curd and Lemon Cheese. A recent import comes from Timaru, New Zealand, and is delicious on bread as well as on cake as a filling between layers. The second butter is simply called Egg Butter. Both keep well.

LEMON BUTTER

In a double boiler, melt ½ cup butter. Stir in grated rind of 2 lemons and ½ cup fresh lemon juice, 1½ cups sugar, a pinch of salt and 4 beaten eggs. Do not allow mixture to boil but keep stirring until mixture thickens. Cool and refrigerate.

EGG BUTTER

Boil 2 cups sugar in ¾ cup water until it forms a thread. Pour a little of this syrup into 2 beaten eggs and then pour into syrup mix. Cook at low heat for 5 minutes. Add your favorite extract – ½ teaspoon. Refrigerate until use.

PREFLAVORED BUTTERS

The likelihood is great that you will be able to buy butter already invested with flavors, at least in the State of California. There, new standards have been adopted for dairy products which permit production and marketing of butter so treated. This means you will be able to buy butter that tastes like syrup, perhaps, as well as butter treated with chives or garlic.

OTHER BREAD SPREADS

Nut butters, made from practically every oily nut, not only taste good but because of their nutritive qualities are often substituted for creamery butter. Among the most nutritious foods known to man, nuts are rich in protein, fats, vitamins, and minerals, especially calcium and phosphorus.

MAKING NUT BUTTER

Nut butter is easy to make with an electric blender. Use shelled, blanched and roasted nuts. Since almonds and cashews are not always roasted, you may have to do this yourself.

NUT BUTTERS

Blend 1 cup of nuts at high speed for a few seconds. Alternate between low and middle speeds thereafter, pushing nuts toward blades with a spatula. Add a few tablespoons of water to make a paste. Remove from blender and salt to taste. Some like to add a little sugar or honey to finish the nut butter.

NUT CREAM SPREAD

Blend ½ cup of nut butter with 1 cup cream cheese, 1 teaspoon fresh lemon juice, 2 teaspoons sugar or honey, and ¼ teaspoon salt.

PEANUT BUTTER

Peanuts lead all other nuts in popularity as the half billion pounds of peanut butter consumed each year demonstrate. The best peanut butter is made largely of Virginia peanuts and half as many Spanish peanuts added to bring up oil content. The greatest breakthrough for the peanut since a physician in St. Louis developed peanut butter in 1890 is a low-calorie product. The trick of making the low-fat peanut butter is to use dry-roasted blanched nuts. This reduces calories from 100 per tablespoon to 43 calories.

LOW CALORIE PEANUT BUTTER

2 cups blanched, dry roasted peanuts
1¼ cups water
2 teaspoons sugar (optional)

Blend peanuts in blender at high speed for several minutes until nuts are powdered. Add water slowly, blending after each addition. Scrape down often with spatula.

Yield: 2¼ cups

Other nuts you can use to make nut butter include acorn, almond, Brazil nut, cashew, hazelnut, pecan, pine nut and walnut.

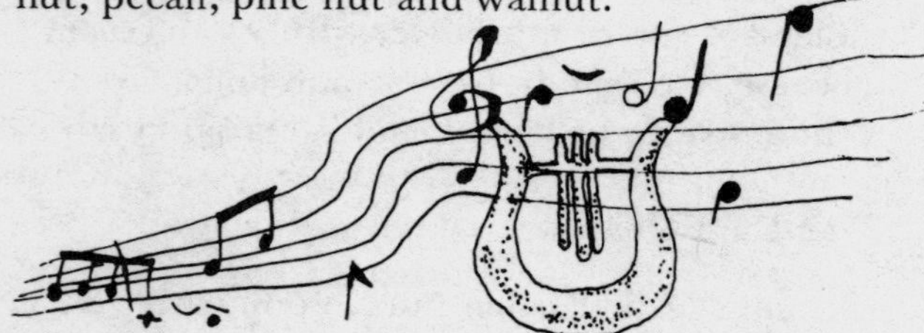

DELIGHTFUL DIVERSITY

Most versatile of all bread spreads are the fruit concoctions. They come to table in seven forms:

Butters, made by cooking fruit pulp with sugar until the mixture is as thick as creamed dairy butter.

Conserves, those jam-like spreads made by boiling two or more fruits with sugar and containing nuts or raisins.

Fruit Honeys, made by cooking grated or finely chopped hard fruits with sugar until they are a little thicker than bee honey.

Jams, made by cooking crushed fruits with sugar until mixture shows little or no free liquid.

Jellies, those clear and sparkling confections made by cooking fruit juice with sugar.

Marmalades, soft jellies containing fruit pulp or peel.

Preserves, confections in which fruit retains its shape, is more or less translucent and plump.

Success in making all these fruit spreads hinges on

1. Using firm ripe fruit of good flavor
2. Weighing fruit after preparing
3. Cooking in small batches
4. Making airtight seals

THANKS TO MONSIEUR APPERT

During the Napoleonic Wars, the French government offered a reward of 12,000 francs to anyone who could develop a satisfactory method of preserving foods for the naval and military stores. M. Appert, brewer, pickler and confectioner, carried off the prize with his wide-necked glass jars and methods of sterilizing and sealing. Thanks to M. Appert and to the screw tops and self-sealing jar lids of Robert Mason and Alexander Kerr, you can preserve the best fruits for your bread spreads.

FRUIT BUTTERS

Fruit butters are made with apples, apricots, bananas, cantaloupes, grapes, lemons, peaches, pears, plums and tomatoes as well as combinations of cantaloupe and peach, blueberry and apple, and apple and quince.

PEAR BUTTER

Wash fruit thoroughly, quarter and remove stems but not cores and skins. Add half as much water as fruit. Cook until fruit is soft, stirring constantly. Press through a colander, then through fine sieve and remove all fibrous material. Quantity of sugar varies according to taste, but is usually half as much sugar as fruit pulp.

Add ¼ to ½ teaspoon salt to each gallon of butter. Boil rapidly and keep stirring to prevent burning. When butter cooks down, reduce heat. Cook until no rim of liquid separates around the edge of the butter. You can add spices to your personal taste.

Pour butter into hot, sterilized glass jars and seal.

CONSERVES

Of all the conserves — and many are a delight we remember best the grape conserves made from Concord grapes and freighted with walnuts.

CONCORD GRAPE CONSERVE

- 2 quarts stemmed grapes
- 6 cups sugar
- 1 cup broken walnuts
- ¼ teaspoon salt

Wash and stem grapes. Press to remove pulps from skins. Run skins through a food chopper, then boil 20 minutes in just enough water to prevent sticking. Cook pulps separately in own juice until soft. Rub through colander to remove seeds. Combine skins and pulps and sugar and boil rapidly until thick. Add salt and nuts that have been heated but not browned. Pour at once into hot sterilized glasses and seal.

Other good fruits for the conserve process include apricots, cranberries, cherries, gooseberries, peaches, pears, prunes and rhubarb. Many introduce lemons and oranges and raisins and a favorite nut ingredient is the blanched almond.

MARMALADES

Marmalades have their followings and many a housewife has collected the distinctive jars in which some of them are sold. Arguments have aired their origin — who, really, was responsible for the confection, the English, the Scots, a French chef or the Portuguese?

The earliest reference to the word dates back to the 16th Century. A conserve of oranges and sugar was made in England in Henry VIII's day, but a storm at sea 200 years later may have been the catalyst that established a sure beachhead for marmalade on the shores of Scotland. A Spanish ship having put ashore at Dundee, its cargo was offered for sale and a grocer bought both sugar and Seville oranges for a song and had them delivered, not to his shop but to his home. His frugal wife whipped out her family recipe for quince marmalet, applied it to the oranges and the rest is history. The marmalade was so popular that the grocer closed up shop and they went into business, founding, in 1797 the House of James Keiller & Son, Ltd.

You can make excellent marmalades from oranges, lemons, grapefruits and about 13 other fruits, at last count. This is to say nothing about marmalades made with carrots, cucumbers and tomatoes.

Here is a way to make orange marmalade that may make you do a lot of standing and waiting, but it will also have your friends standing in line to have a gift of a small jar of it.

ORANGE MARMALADE

3 medium oranges
1 medium lemon
3 quarts cold water
Sugar, about 8 cups

Carefully wash and dry fruit. Do not peel. Thinly slice into half circles. Combine orange and lemon slices and water in a large glass bowl. Cover and let stand 12 hours or overnight.

Place in deep, heavy saucepan and bring to boil. Boil hard for 30 minutes, until reduced to about 8 cups.

Let stand another 6 to 8 hours. Measure fruit and liquid and add an equal amount of sugar. Bring to boil, stirring until sugar dissolves. Boil rapidly until mixture sheets from spoon when tested, about 30 minutes. Stir occasionally to avoid sticking. Remove from heat. Stir and skim for 5 minutes. Pour into hot sterilized glass jars and seal.

AND IF YOU HAVE A FREEZER

If you have ever tasted jams and jellies that are frozen, you may elect never to prepare them any other way. They have that unutterably fresh sweetness that just picked fruits impart. They will keep several weeks at refrigerator temperatures or several months in a freezer.

The family expert in these matters has been spoiling us for years with frozen jams she makes in Oregon with boysenberries, nectarberries, strawberries, raspberries, sweet cherries and blackberries.

"I don't cook the fruit at all," she tells us. "Simply measure the fruit — 3½ cups — and squash it — or grind it if it happens to be pitted sweet cherries. Add a little lemon juice and pour in a package of powdered pectin."

She has her favorite brand and you probably have yours!

"I stir the pectin into the fruit thoroughly and let it stand for 30 minutes, stirring occasionally. Then I add a cup of white corn syrup to keep the sugar from crystallizing. Sugar comes next, 2 cups of sugar to each cup of fruit. I stir it and stir it and stir it until all the sugar is dissolved. Then it goes straight into containers, I cap them and put them right in the freezer. They keep indefinitely in the deep freeze. I have some in jelly glasses. When I want some jam or jelly for toast, I take out what I want and put the rest back in the freezer."

It's as simple as that.

Now you have it all — bread, butter and jam. You know how easy they are to make. You know what is in them.

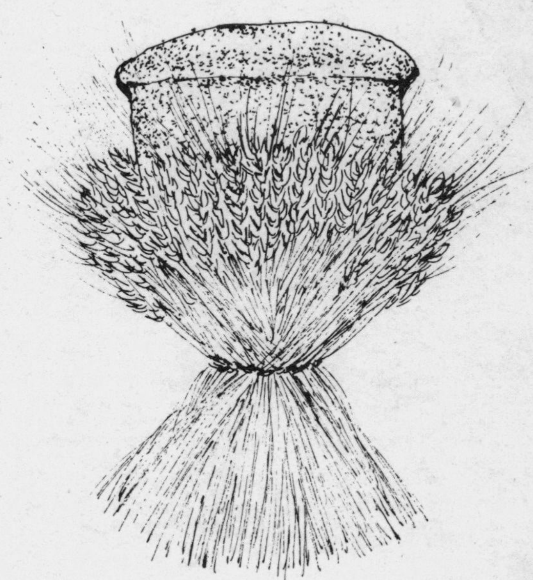

INDEX OF RECIPES

Recipes That Should Be Kept

notes from your own Experiences, Experiments, & Explorations